"It is great to read a book whic ... rs really understand the many ne ... ed from effective and thoughtful r ...

Even if you choose not to grov ... ss networking, there's so much va ... of 'givers gain' that you can use in other areas of prospecting.

As a way of being, 'givers gain'® can help you to win in so many areas of your life - not just your business.

Moreover, I'm pleased that two minds like Wes and Stefan have joined together, with their considerable areas of expertise in their own space, to work on a book that will help network marketers get the best out of their networking groups, which in turn will help the other members win too."

Ivan Misner, Founder & Chief Visionary Officer of BNI Worldwide

"So many skills for business success crammed in here, whether you go to formal networking events or simply within your circle of influence. I always love Wes Linden's books and recommend them to my team, and I know how highly Wes rates Stefan Thomas, so I'm delighted to see them collaborating on this book that *will* become a classic! Good work Wes and Stefan!"

Natalie Heeley, Top Ranking Network Marketing Leader

"These networking kings have cracked the formula of how to get business networking to work for network marketers! If you're serious about creating opportunities, growing your team and making real sales from your networking, this book has been written for you - it's essential reading."

Brad Burton, Founder of 4Networking

"After briefly talking to our family and friends, the rest of our network marketing career will be networking with new people. Let Wes and Stefan teach and guide you for the best ways to network your business to success. Learn to get others to refer great prospects to you."

Tom 'Big Al' Schreiter, Network Marketing Legend

"Whether you are shy and unassuming, or a gregarious, outgoing person, you'll learn a lot from this book. It is a 'Master Class' on networking."

Randy Gage, Author of the New York Times bestsellers, Risky Is the New Safe and Mad Genius

"As his upline, I have watched Wes build a very successful Network Marketing business over the last two decades. I get many comments on his skilled ability to network, as well as to tell interesting, relevant and compelling stories.

This book is skilfully written by Wes and Stefan and is a must-read."

Steve Critchley, Top Ranking Network Marketing Leader & International Speaker

"Stefan has mastered the art of effective networking in a traditional business setting. Wes has mastered building a network marketing business.

So, I'm excited to see a book that combines their skills and knowledge to help network marketers generate greater results when it comes to expanding their influence in whatever environment they're looking to grow their business."

Barry 'The Book' Phillips, Founder of KnowledgeisKing.co.uk

"Wes and Stefan have put together one of the most complete guides to networking that I have ever read. Some consider networking 'old-school' but the truth is, those with a large network of solid professionals and business people have the largest circle of influence. And circle of influence will make or break any business. This easy to read book, in my opinion, is THE GUIDE TO MODERN NETWORKING. It digs into some of the simple, but mostly overlooked, idiosyncrasies of networking, including your approach, what to do and not to do, what to wear, how to prepare and even what to bring with you! This is must read for the professional networker. Thanks for writing this book Wes and Stefan!"

Jordan Adler, Network Marketing Leader & Author of the Best-Selling book 'Beach Money'

"Network Marketing is a conversation. Actually, it's two conversations: The Networking conversation, and the Marketing conversation.

Ask yourself, on a scale of one to 10, with 10 being 'Couldn't be better' and one being 'Utterly pathetic', how do you rate your own Networking and Marketing conversations (and thanks for your honesty!)?

Now, when you've read Wes and Stefan's book three times - race through the first time, deliberately do the second, and study for the exam on the third - rate yourself again, one to 10. I'll bet you the cover price of the book you're higher by two to four points.

And THAT's what a book like this is supposed to give you. Wes and Stefan are superb been-there, done-that, show you how teachers. Great book!"

John Milton Fogg, Author of the million-selling book 'The Greatest Networker in the World.'

"Having worked closely with Stefan for several years, and more recently with Wes, I was delighted to be asked to review their new book. I thought I'd do so over a couple of evenings, you know, take my time over it. The reality was I started to read it and then couldn't stop!

I'm heavily involved in networking and network up to four or five times a week for my business, so you'd think I'd got this networking thing nailed, right?

Wow - this book hit me with knowledge bombs in every chapter - networking nuggets of gold that I can start to use right now to make a difference to my business."

Sheena Whyatt, Business Networking Regional Leader and Founder of KAPOW Personal Branding Training

"When it comes down to becoming a 'go to' person, Wes and Stefan are leading by example in this field. By reading these simple principles you can make a huge impact in your business."

Payam Moghim, Network Marketing Corporate Training Consultant for the Middle East

"I'm a great believer in following the path of the greats.

Stefan is someone I've long admired for his honest and simple approach to business networking. Wes is one of those guys who you think would be more aloof and less contactable given his huge success in network marketing. But, like Stef, he's a really down-to-earth guy and the advice, chats, and content I've had from him over the years have been a valuable part of my business education.

This book is a little business gem! It's set to be one of those classic books that Small Medium Enterprise owners read and will recommend.

If you're about to set out, or are already on the exciting but lonely road to success in business, then you should follow that road with

Stef and Wes in this step-by-step book.

Banks should hand this beautifully laid-out book out as standard protocol to everyone who sets up a business. It's that important you have this information because it'll save years of wasted time in networking meetings and generate you more meaningful business connections and opportunities to grow.

Enjoy this entertaining and educational read, but most importantly follow what is set down in it word-for-word. This is the business networking gospel of our time.

Stef and Wes are networking pros and this book is a brilliant read you simply can't (and won't) put down. This is a gift to the business world. Take it."

Social Media Todd, Business Networking Group Leader and Founder of Spaghetti Social Media Agency

"Having worked closely on different projects with both Wes and Stefan, I know that they have a huge amount of valuable content to bring to the table.

If you're looking to build your home-based business, read this book carefully to help you understand how you can flourish in either a business networking enivronment, or by simply putting into action those skills to increase your influence within your own space, and thus increase your income."

Paul Goundry, Head of Training for a FTSE250 PLC

"Most people talk too much. What they say is disorganised, self-obsessed, and bores the people they are in front of. Learning how to present yourself, your message, and win the room takes discipline and hard work.

Luckily Wes and Stefan help you find the shortcut to getting a successful result when you're looking to grow your business, whether in a formal networking setting, or simply in and around the people you naturally come into contact with.

Learn how to be the one that makes an impact, by getting results with the gems contained within this book."

Mark Davis, Best-Selling Author of 'Excite, Engage and Entertain'

WIN THE ROOM

FROM BEST-SELLING AUTHORS

WES LINDEN AND STEFAN THOMAS

How to become a 'go to' person to achieve network marketing success, using simple principles from business networking

NOAH'S HOUSE PUBLISHING

Published by Noah's House Publishing
www.noahshousepublishing.com

A CIP catalogue record for this book is available from the British Library
Print Book: ISBN 978-1-910138-37-3

Published by Noah's House Publishing
www.noahshousepublishing.com
All enquiries to enquiries@noahshousepublishing.com

Proof-read by Michelle Emerson, Graeme Linden and Alex Johnson
Cover design by Dan Debnam
Tea-making by Josh Hollands

Typeset by Biddles Books, Blackborough End, King's Lynn, Norfolk
Printed and bound in Great Britain by Lightning Source

Contents

Introductions

HELLO FROM WES!

I was that guy.

Yep - the one who was ***so*** enamoured with my network marketing product, and opportunity, that my early days in business networking were spent believing that people were waking up early, driving to a random golf club or hotel, paying for breakfast and membership, just so I could sell to them.

I was positive that they were certain to beg me to 'sign them up' for my products, and at the same time they were sure to jump away from their chosen profession and become a 24/7, fully-committed Distributor with my network marketing opportunity.

And I just knew that swarming around the room at speed, thrusting cards into the hands of everyone I saw was going to be a highly effective way to get the phone ringing off the hook.

It was a disaster!

I got no referrals, no customers, no team members, and nobody wanting to speak to me at the meetings.

Thankfully, I took the hint pretty quickly.

How many of us recognise this approach, either from our own early days or from team members we have introduced? Whether it is in a business networking environment, or at a family party, in the canteen at work, at a local show, at the school gates, in our party plan events, or on social media.

By nature, I am the giving type, so this desperate and grabby approach was not really in my character. It was just that nobody bothered to explain to me that it wasn't like *Supermarket Sweep* where you only had 60 seconds to grab as much as you could. So, it didn't take me more than a couple of weeks of this disastrous approach, and a quiet word of friendly advice from a stalwart of the business networking group, to change my approach to something much more palatable and, within months, I was probably the most referred person in the room.

So, what has this got to do with you?

I'm fairly sure that those reading this will fall into three camps:

The person I described above is you!

You're actually really good at networking and you're already making a success of it.

You haven't even contemplated business networking, and you're not sure if it is for you but whether it is or isn't there's still a myriad of skills you could learn from this area of lead-generation and relationship building.

If you're in the first camp, fear not. We're here to help. Both Stefan and I see far too many really keen people make a total, utter disaster of business networking, simply because they were too eager, too enthusiastic and didn't understand how to make it work for them. Even if you don't currently fish with this rod, you'll learn the skills from people who have mastered networking in a significant way, which has ensured they become the 'go to' person, and that, my friends, will be good for you however you approach people.

When I first met Stefan, one of our initial conversations was about how badly some really good people do in the business networking environment. How this was leading to some very credible businesses being spoken about disrespectfully, and creating uncomfortable pre-judgements for too many Distributors further down the line.

Maybe you're in camp two. Don't get me wrong - not everyone gets it wrong. And it's not just network marketers who fluff it up. Some of you reading this will have already proved to be perfectly capable in this environment. You should keep reading because I am confident you will still find some gems that will help you improve your results and, significantly, the content contained within will help you support your team members who don't have your natural flair for business networking.

If you're in camp three, be assured that the tips contained within this book will help you in your day-to-day network marketing business, irrespective of whether you ever start business networking yourself. It may, of course, also inspire you to find a group and add this to your strategy to grow your business.

Most of what it takes to succeed in this environment and win the room over is about you making a really good impression with people in your community, and there'll be many ideas you can steal and use to support you in your business. Plus, you will have team members in the future who want to succeed in business networking, and if you haven't done it, you'll still be well-placed to offer them a perspective and some insight based on what is contained within.

As Stefan and I got to know each other better, it became really obvious to me that between us we had some insights and skills that could be hugely beneficial to those in the network marketing space who want to grow their business through business networking. Stefan is a well-renowned speaker, leading authority and trainer in the business networking space, and so it was great for me to work with him to bring you content that will genuinely help network marketers achieve more.

Whether you read this book as someone in the first, second or third camp, I'm confident that if you action what you learn, you'll never be that guy or gal who people avoid. You've got a great chance of becoming the most referred person in the room and, even if you never take up business networking, you'll still put this book down having learned some great tips which will support you in other areas of your business.

HELLO FROM STEFAN!

One of my biggest frustrations, along with being middle-aged and overweight, comes from spotting people making little mistakes in networking, which, if corrected, could make a massive difference to their success.

Over the ten years or so I've been on this networking journey I've seen so many decent people dismiss networking because they tried it a few times and it didn't 'work' for them. I think my biggest frustration, and undoubtedly theirs, is watching people from the same business achieve demonstrable success from their networking efforts - leaving them wondering where on earth they went wrong.

Two people, from similar backgrounds, in the same network marketing organisation, attending networking meetings organised by the same networking organisation, can have such wildly different results - why is that?

I acknowledge that I have some advantages. In 1983, aged 13, I started working in the gent's department of a shoe shop, as a Saturday boy. It was a busy department in a busy store and I enjoyed it immensely. The one and only incentive we were offered, on top of our 99p per hour wages, was that the person who sold the most fancies on a Saturday got to go home half an hour early, leaving at 5:30 rather than 6pm.

Fancies, if you've never worked in the shoe business, are the upsells - for example, polish, Scotchgard, shoe trees, that sort of thing.

My bus, so that this makes some sense to you, left at 20 minutes to the hour. So, if I left at 5:30 I got the 5:40 bus. If I left at 6, I got the 6:40 bus. That half an hour was actually worth an hour to me.

So, this 13-year-old, in my grey trousers, lemon shirt and matching tie, got good at selling fancies. Really good. And, as a result, I got to go home early most Saturdays. I was the guy who was popular with the management, but less so with my colleagues, who were left to sweep up.

I realise now, some 35 years later, that those skills which I learned to sell fancies are still useful to me today. What I teach people in networking is pretty similar to what I taught myself back then.

Selling fancies was all about starting a conversation. *"Were you looking for anything in particular, sir?"* and then, once the conversation was open, using the 20 minutes I had with that customer to build the relationship to the extent that they trusted me when I offered them a suitable addition to their purchase. It was also about, of course, actually offering them the opportunity of buying an additional product - something which most of my colleagues failed to do.

Being brave enough to approach a customer, talking to them, building rapport, serving them, not prejudging whether they would or wouldn't buy any fancies, and closing the sale. All of these were things which would sell a £1.79 tin of Scotchgard on top of the £19.99 brogues the gentleman had just chosen.

I know, and have proven both personally and with my private clients, that we can apply a similar process to networking. I also know that, applied correctly, the same principles can be applied to growing your network marketing business using networking as a marketing tool.

I also know, which is fundamental, that anyone can be trained to do this stuff successfully. It has nothing to do with someone's work or educational background and in networking (as in network marketing) everyone starts as the new boy or girl, no matter what they were doing before.

I had heard of Wes Linden and his success in network marketing over many years. A series of pretty random events led to us getting to know each other as friends. I read his books, he read my books, and saw that we had a lot in common. I would talk about building relationships and allowing serendipity to take over, Wes would talk about making friends for the sake of making friends.

We were, quite simply, using slightly different language but with exactly the same philosophy – long-term, strong, mutually beneficial relationships beat the hard sell every time. Along the way, the idea to collaborate on a book popped up and so, here we are.

There is nobody I would rather write a book aimed at network marketers, owners of home-based businesses and anyone involved in direct selling with. Wes is, in my opinion, the 21st century voice of network marketing and I know the value he has put into the sections of this book he has written. They have the potential to transform your business IF, of course, you actually act on what you read.

The reason I've spent over a year writing this book alongside Wes is that I want one more person to be successful in their networking and network marketing.

If you read this book, and apply even some of what Wes and I have written, you get to choose whether that one person is you.

Chapter 1

Why, where and when - Getting started with networking events

Stefan Thomas

Whilst the content and skills in this book will help network marketers grow their standing in the areas that they choose to promote their business, whether at the school gates, with friends and family, amongst work colleagues, through home launches or party plan events, online posts or demo videos or a collection of all these things, we are taking a deep dive into the business networking world. It's a huge space that many people overlook, have never heard of, or perhaps feel they shouldn't consider. But with so many incredible success stories from this area of prospecting, we will certainly be taking a deep dive into the world of business networking so that you are better placed to make a decision; whether or not it is something you will add to your armoury, and so you can credibly advise team members in the future when they ask about it.

Let's go!

Why every network marketer should go to business networking events.

Where to find business networking events.

How to find the 'right' networking events for you and your network marketing business.

Why?

Before I started going to networking events I had never heard of network marketing, and I think that's a much more important point than we maybe recognise.

In our own little worlds, whether that is a network marketing organisation or a business networking group, it is difficult to believe that people haven't come across the network marketing profession before. We become so engrossed in what we know, and what we believe the world to be like, that we forget that there are many, many people outside of our bubble.

So, think about that again. Before I started attending business networking events, I had no preconceptions of network marketing, because the concept had never been introduced to me. The various network marketing organisations prevalent in the UK, and the entire concept of network marketing, had never been in my world before, and now they were.

Business networking offers an enviable opportunity to meet business owners who may be completely new to the concept of network marketing, but that isn't the only reason to consider attending networking events, and certainly shouldn't be the overriding reason.

For any business to succeed, including any network marketing business, having a network of other professionals around that business isn't just important, it is vital to the success of the business. Not everyone in that network will become a customer or client, but everyone in that network has value. Some will become suppliers, some will become friends, some will become confidantes and advisers, and some will, of course, become clients and customers. Business networking events give any business the opportunity to fast-track the building of that network, and create a network of the right type of people.

But even that isn't the only benefit of getting into the world of networking. Every networking group I have been to, and every networking organisation I have been part of, has been supportive and keen for everyone in the group to succeed. The opportunity to introduce new business ideas, try out new ways of introducing the business, launch new products and services and just generally benefit from a supportive network, is massively undervalued. And just being around other business people who understand self-employment is worthwhile in itself.

When I first joined a business networking group, I thought there would be a whole load of people there waiting to buy from me. In fairness, that was pretty much how it was introduced to me. That didn't happen, not immediately at least, and over time I have learnt the many other benefits of being in a networking group, as well as the many opportunities which networking groups offer to their members.

Hopefully this chapter will give you some ideas around why you should look at business networking as a way to grow your business, as well as some practical advice around how and where to find the right networking groups for you and your business.

Before I go any further, and before you message me to tell me, I do know that there are other ways of growing your network marketing business. And I do know that there are some, if not many, people in network marketing around the world who never attend a business networking event. So, I know it can be done, and has been done. And I actually think that those people who have been so successful could have been even more successful if they had added business networking to their armoury. Whether you choose to get started with business networking or not, you'll learn some great skills and ideas from this book to add to your repertoire that will help you with the other ways you use to grow your business.

Every business should consider multiple ways of marketing their products and services, network marketing businesses no less so. And business networking, as well as all the other benefits it offers, is a valuable and efficient way to market your business.

Network marketing millionaire Jordan Adler, the author of the highly-acclaimed best-selling book '*Beach Money*' has used networking to help him build his business and he said the following:

"I was introduced to my first networking event about 13 years ago.

It was a small group and I was brand new in my business. They went around the room and asked each person to do a 30 second commercial. Afterwards I had a handful of people hand me their business cards with an invitation to follow up with them. I learned that this organization, BNI, had chapters all over the world and I immediately saw a huge opportunity! I figured that as I grew my team, if I just promoted this networking organization within my network marketing network, I would eventually have distributors in chapters all over world.

Instant customers and the leverage of a worldwide network.

The meetings were already set up and there were people in attendance each week that would work to promote our business as long as we did our best to promote theirs! It was a marriage made in heaven!

Over the next 10 years, I added over 30,000 distributors and 100,000 customers to my business as a result of my relationship with this organisation.

I have three pieces of advice to anyone interested in using these types of networking opportunities to grow their business:

1) Plan to find a good chapter and attend their meetings weekly. Building trust and getting to know the other members is the most important component to success.

2) Focus on finding ways to help and add value to the other members of the group. The philosophy is "Giver's Gain"®.

3) Don't sell to the other members. Build trust by teaching the others (your sales team) how they can help you. Referrals are your lifeblood."

Where?

If you've never been to a networking event before, you may not know where to find them, but it is usually quite simple.

Pretty much every town in the world has at least one business networking group, and most have several. Business owners like to network, to share opportunities, knowledge and just to get to know each other. Every local economy benefits from some sort of networking activity so even if you don't know where to look yet, they are there.

In the UK there are several national networking organisations who are represented in most towns. Even if they aren't represented, they may offer you the chance to get involved in setting up one of their groups.

In no particular order, these are some of the networking organisations you will come across the UK:

BNI - BNI are the world's largest referral marketing organisation. There are chapters in most towns and cities in the UK and each chapter is restricted to only having one member from each profession, trade or industry. You can find more details, and look up your nearest chapter, on their website at www.bni.co.uk.

4Networking - 4Networking run over 5,000 networking meetings every year and any member can attend any meeting anywhere in the UK. You can find details of your nearest meeting, along with membership options and other details, on their website at www.4networking.biz.

Business Biscotti - Biscotti run networking events in various locations across the UK and their members can attend any group, anywhere. Their website contains details of locations, and the benefits of joining, at www.businessbiscotti.co.uk.

Business Over Breakfast - BoB Clubs, as they are known, exist in several countries and, in the UK, in various locations. Their groups offer meetings every fortnight, and their members refer business to each other. Locations and more details can be found at www.bobclubs.com.

The Athena Network - Athena describes itself as 'The Premier Networking Organisation for Women In Business' and offers various groups and membership options. Full details are on their website at www.theathenanetwork.co.uk.

As well as the national networking organisations, most towns have local independent groups too. Asking your existing business contacts is often the easiest way to find local groups, but if that doesn't help, a quick Google search will. In some areas, you may even find networking events for parents with toddlers over a play date.

Googling 'networking groups YOURTOWN', or 'networking events YOURTOWN' or 'business networking YOURTOWN' will at least give you a start on what's out there.

Aside from that, it is likely that your local Chamber of Trade or Commerce will offer some sort of networking, and very often the members of other networking groups can be found there too. You can find details of your local chamber at www.britishchambers.org.uk.

By the way, if you ever thought that networking events only take place on a weekday early morning, allow me to correct you. You can find events taking place early morning before work, after the school run, brunch, lunch, afternoon tea, drinks, cheese and wine, supper, you name it, you can find it.

Membership (paid for) and non-membership groups

Some networking groups charge for membership, whereas some charge you only for each meeting you attend and others are even completely free to attend. So, what's the difference and why on earth would you pay to attend when you could do so for free?

Organisations such as Athena, BNI, 4Networking and others are national or international organisations which charge business owners to be members. They may even have a certain set of criteria you have to achieve before you can apply to be a member. Broadly speaking these organisations have benefits over and above the 'free' networking groups. The benefits might be national or international reach, training in networking skills, your business listed on their website, discounts on business services and others. There is also typically a charge when you attend each meeting.

Some organisations are free to be a member of, you only pay when you attend - such as Biscotti. These too offer benefits and are well worth checking out. Some events are completely free to attend, typically because they have arranged sponsorship.

My preference is the networking organisations you have to pay for, although I know some people prefer to join the free to attend groups. My experience has been that people who have invested in their networking are keener to get a return on it, and therefore put more effort into their networking skills and things such as looking for referrals. The free to attend events are typically sponsored, so often the ten or fifteen minute presentation isn't anything educational, but a sales pitch from the sponsor, which is completely understandable as they've just paid for your sandwiches.

My advice, as always, is to try several, and pick the one which suits you, your personality and your business. There is no 'one size fits all'.

How?

With all of this opportunity though, how do you find the group which will work for you? There is almost too much out there, and I understand that it might be overwhelming to someone new to networking to identify the 'right' group or groups.

There is no simple or absolute answer to this, as the choice of which group or groups is 'right' will always be subjective. This is my advice, based on my experience and the experience of the hundreds of people I've worked with over the years.

And it is pretty simple. Try each group out for size. Experience them, see if you can get to know the people, and decide whether you feel comfortable there.

If you are going to make networking work, you're going to be spending a fair amount of time around the people in the group, and with the format of that group. So, it is vitally important that you are not only comfortable being there, but enjoy being there too. You are hardly likely to apply yourself if you don't like the group or the people.

The national groups mentioned above all offer the chance to come along as a visitor at least once, before you have to make a commitment to join. And most local groups aren't membership based, so you can turn up a few times, or as often as you like, before deciding whether or not it is for you.

Chapter 2

Getting your ducks in a row - What you do before the event

Stefan Thomas

So, you've found the perfect networking event, you've booked in, got it in your diary, all you need do now is just turn up and meet people, right?

That is, in truth, what most people do, and it is possible to have some success by doing just that. It is marginally better than not going to a networking meeting at all. But a small amount of preparation and advanced planning, and just thinking about how you are going to approach the event, can and will make a huge difference.

In this chapter, we will look at what and how to prepare for a networking event, to give you a competitive advantage as soon as you arrive. Even if networking meetings aren't for you, there are plenty of principles you can steal and apply to your own activities.

Expectations

When people plan for networking events, particularly if they are relatively new to networking, I find that they very often set their expectations way too high, and thus come away disappointed. Sounds like every other type of prospecting, huh?! So, it is worth spending a few moments thinking about that, and what a realistic expectation might be.

Remember that the networking event itself is only the start of the conversation, and your goal is to start conversations which you can then take forward after the event. People sometimes try to make the networking event the whole of the conversation and try to achieve a sale right there and then. Take that pressure off and consider how you would react if someone you had only just met tried immediately to sell to you. You wouldn't like it, right? Neither will they, so don't try.

Instead, look to each networking event to increase the number of conversations you have started and to take some more conversations forward. Instead of setting a goal based on how much you will sell, just think about starting new relationships. The number of conversations you start is less important than the quality of those relationships, and how much you are getting to know people.

So, prepare your expectations first, set the bar low for each networking event, but set the bar high for how much effort you will put into developing those relationships.

People not prospects

Something which I think is often confusing about networking meetings is the expectation of why everyone else is there.

You're going there for the sake of your business, right? Everyone else is there for the same reason - for the sake of their own business. So, you're not walking into a room full of prospects for you, you're walking into a room full of people who are concerned with growing their own business first. No different to when you go to a BBQ or school play or log onto social media - the people you are interacting with have turned up for a very different reason than to be pitched to, so the key thing is to start the conversations that lead to the next one. That isn't to say that some of them won't become prospects, but they haven't attended the networking meeting just to buy from you, and it is vital that you don't treat them as such.

Using social media to meet people before the event

Social media is an absolutely fantastic tool for making sure that you never have to walk into a room full of people who you don't know, ever again.

You can, and should, use social media to connect with attendees before the event, engage with them, and allow people to get to know you, before you arrive.

Here's how to do it.

Some networking groups publish details of their attendees either on their website, or by sending out a list of attendees prior to the event. Using this you can search for the attendees on Twitter, tell them you're looking forward to meeting them, and allow the conversation to go from there.

If the event or organisation doesn't publish a list, you may have to get a little more creative. Using search on Twitter and Facebook, look for the name of the event and see who is talking about it. This is significantly easier on Twitter as there is more of a culture of engaging with people you're not connected with, but on Facebook you may find a page for the event, or just be able to 'like' someone's comment that they're attending.

Either way, once you know who is there, you can look them up on LinkedIn, as well as Twitter and Facebook, and let the conversation start before you even get to the event.

Your networking toolkit

What do you need to take to a networking event? Have the organisers given you any clues in their confirmation email or call?

This list is neither meant to be comprehensive, nor mandatory. You don't have to take any of these items to a networking event but, in my opinion, they will help you to get the most out of the event.

Business cards - bit of a no-brainer this. Even in the electronic age people still expect you to have a business card with your contact details on it. One tip on this, if you want to be taken seriously as a business person, treat your business seriously and invest a little bit of money in your cards. Do not go to networking events with cards which announce on the back that they were printed for free by an online printing service - it gives the impression you're not prepared to invest in your business, so why should anyone else?

Something to make notes on and in - you're likely to have a lot of conversations at a networking event and, hopefully, some of those conversations will result in follow-up actions. I try to pretend I'm very modern and cool so make all my notes electronically (famously, I'm a big fan of Evernote and even wrote my contribution to this book using that platform). You may prefer pen and paper. It ultimately doesn't matter how you make notes, as long as you do. No matter how much you trust your memory, it will let you down, so have a system to record what was said, and, crucially, what you said you would do, and then do it.

Leaflets or brochures - Every networking meeting I have ever been to has some way for attendees to display leaflets, brochures or other promotional material. If you have any it is worth taking them, if you don't, it is worth getting some printed - it doesn't need to cost the earth. You never know, that one person you weren't able to talk to might be interested in something on your leaflet or brochure. It is very passive marketing, but if it is there for the duration of the meeting it is possible it will catch someone's eye.

Pop-up or roller banners - many networking meetings give their attendees the opportunity to display a roller banner or pop-up banner. Once again, these don't need to cost the earth and are a particularly useful way of having your contact details on display throughout the meeting.

Your diary - I carry my diary around on my iPhone and other devices so I don't have to make a choice here. But if you have a paper diary, it is absolutely worth having it with you at every networking meeting. If you have *THAT* conversation where the other person is really keen on what you do and wants to move things forward, then if you have your diary available you can strike whilst the iron is hot and get a follow-on meeting booked in straight away. We will talk about this much more, later in the book, but the sooner you move on something the more likely people are to do it. The longer you leave your follow-up, the more chance there is that someone will forget why they wanted the next meeting with you. Carry your diary, and then get those follow-on meetings booked at the earliest opportunity.

What to wear

I know that this subject vexes and causes a degree of anxiety in a lot of people. Will everyone else be wearing a suit? Is it ok to be casual? Is there some sort of dress code that I've not been told about?

Let's hope I can allay some of those fears here.

Firstly, if there is a dress code, the organisers will tell you. And if they haven't told you, get in touch with them and ask. If you are at all worried, then being in touch and at least having an answer will help you to worry less.

But shock, horror! What if they say there isn't a dress code? What then? It's a bit like dress-down Friday at work, is it really dress-down or is there still some sort of expectation?

These days, sort of famously in my world, I attend most networking meetings and speaking engagements in jeans and a suitably loud shirt. To some extent that has become my uniform. I get away with it now, even at events where everyone else is wearing a suit but, if you're attending your first networking meeting, it isn't what I would recommend.

I remember an event sometime in the 1990s where I was badly advised about the dress code. I arrived in chinos and a polo shirt (different times) to find that out of 400 people there, 399 were wearing navy or grey suits. It was a swelteringly hot English summer's day, it was an outside event, I was by far the most suitably dressed, but I wanted the ground to open up and allow me to just disappear into it. I didn't have the confidence in those days to be the one to stand out.

At most networking events, it is perfectly acceptable these days to wear what you would normally wear for your normal working day. However, if you're attending for the first time, I would suggest that before you confirm the lack of dress code, and before you are comfortable enough to wear whatever you want, it is better to be overdressed at first rather than face the discomfort of being underdressed.

Once you're in, once you know a few people there and feel a little more relaxed, then you can decide to dress however you feel comfortable; but I would still recommend playing it safe at first.

After that, of course, your choice will depend on how you want to be perceived. Plenty of people in my networking circles still prefer to dress very formally or conservatively as they like that 'professional' look. On the other hand, I prefer to dress how I am most comfortable, whilst some people decide they want to make a distinct impression. A friend of mine used to wear a purple silk suit matched with purple crocs. It was difficult to ignore his presence in the room.

In any case, whether you are going for the first time, or are a long-standing networker, it is worth putting a little thought into how you want to look.

Planning your time

I am a huge advocate of getting to networking meetings early. If they advertise a 7:30 for 8 start, I will be the person there at 7:30. Equally, I will always leave time in my diary after the meeting and never plan to leave as soon as it finishes at 10.

The opportunity to use the extra time at the beginning to have more conversations with other attendees is hugely overlooked. Being there early gives you the chance to chat to the organisers before anyone else arrives, and to meet people as they come in, plus it gives you first dibs on the tea and coffee.

I have always intended to get to networking meetings early and make the best use of my time there. Every big opportunity starts with a little conversation and it is often in those little conversations before the meeting officially starts that I have found, or created, the biggest opportunities.

At the very least, if you have planned to be there early and there are problems with traffic or parking, you have given yourself a useful buffer, rather than arriving late and flustered.

I also leave plenty of time immediately after the meeting so I don't have to rush off to my next appointment. This gives me the flexibility to have an immediate and impromptu one-to-one with someone I have met, if we need to continue the conversation.

Even if there isn't anyone to have a one-to-one with, this is the ideal time to review your notes and plan, or even better execute, your follow-up activities. I can often be found at the end of a meeting scanning in or entering business card details into my CRM, and then firing off those follow-up emails as well as connecting with my new contacts across social media, straight away. That way, your new contacts will receive your follow-up whilst your meeting is still fresh in their minds too, rather than days later when they've started to forget about the great conversation you had.

By the way, if you're not familiar with a 'CRM' it stands for 'customer relationship management' and is where I choose to record details of the people who I meet, and set tasks for myself to follow up with them.

My goal in writing this chapter is not to give you loads more to do, but to help ensure that your time spent at networking meetings is as comfortable and productive as possible. Just putting some thought into your preparation will save you huge amounts of time in the long run, just as being prepared in any of your prospecting endeavours or social situations is going to be more effective than leaving it to chance.

Chapter 3

Making the right impression, every time

Wes Linden

We are being judged by everything we do. From when we arrive at a networking event to when we leave, our colleagues are judging us. Likewise, we are judging others too, but this book is about us, not them!

When I was actively attending networking events on a regular basis, I took the view that people have a choice whether to like and trust me, dislike and distrust me, or be ambivalent. I wanted them to like and trust me. Thus, I worked hard to consider all elements of my involvement and interaction with the group. To build upon what Stefan shared in the previous chapter, here are some key lessons I can share from my networking events that can easily be utilised into your own approach, whether that is formal networking or your other rainmaker activities.

Making a good first impression

I was not necessarily the very first person to arrive, but I was certainly one of the earliest and rather than just help myself to a cup of tea and then standing there on my own supping it, I would be sure to check if the committee members and helpers needed an extra pair of hands for anything. Often, they didn't, but it always surprised me how many people turned up and did not do this. I certainly don't encourage us to appear sycophantic or like an excitable puppy, as that's likely to irritate people, but basic manners and consideration have never done anyone any harm. The simple courtesy of offering some help when there was no obligation to do so, to my mind, gave me some early goodwill.

I would always ensure I was parked appropriately and my car was clean. How often I would see people in dirty vehicles, especially noticeable when they're branded, was shocking. At one group I went to, a lazy and disrespectful culture developed where members would park in the disabled spaces. They took the view that it was closer to the entrance and on the basis that no disabled people were in the group - and at seven o'clock in the morning it would be unlikely that someone who was genuinely in need of the space would be coming for lunch or an evening meal.

As I saw it, they missed a number of really basic points with this behaviour, that certainly made me reticent to refer them and ensured others spoke badly of them also.

Firstly, it's basic good manners for people who don't require a disabled parking space, to not park in it. When you choose to go against this, you get people's backs up and appear disrespectful.

Secondly, what if one of the guests requires the space? I would be fairly sure they wouldn't come back to a group where members were that selfish, and at least it would most certainly create a terrible first impression.

Thirdly, in my mind it represents a contemptuous flippancy which left me (and others) asking *'if they can be this discourteous over something like this, then how will their approach to business be, and can I trust them with my friends?'*

You may now wonder why I'm speaking for so long about a disabled parking space, however, the three questions I pose above are representative of many different behaviours we may see at networking that could turn people off us, or indeed, when we go to an appointment or do anything that brings us into contact with prospects, customers or team members.

Do we jump the queue for food? Do we fill our plate too high from the buffet and not leave enough for others? Are we impatient or rude to the waiting staff? Do we continuously text or play on social media when others are talking? Are we dressed appropriately for the group we are attending? Do we smell of cigarette smoke? Are our fingernails and shoes clean? Are we gossiping or bitching about other members, which always creates the question as to whether we'll be doing the same later on about those we are talking to?

Tristan Lee, author of the book *'Munch, Move, Moisturise: How to Age Gorgeously in Your 30s, 40s, 50s and Beyond'* is well-known on social media as 'The Gorgeousness Coach'. He's the guy that is famed for being nearly 50 but he still gets asked for ID when buying alcohol! But he has also grown a successful network marketing team and has attended many networking meetings.

Here he shares his top five personal care tips to keep in mind when you want to make a great first impression:

"People judge a book by its cover, so taking that bit of extra effort to make that cover appealing is a great way to make a really positive first impression. Whilst I appreciate many people looking to build a business take heed of these tips, I also noticed on my own networking travels that many seem not to!

1. Fresh breath: few things create a worse initial impact than breath that smells like the inside of a garbage can! Keep chewing gum and mints to hand at all times and avoid spicy food, garlic and cigarettes to ensure maximum fresh breath fabulousness.

2. Clean teeth: if you want people to focus on your message and not what's between your teeth then always check them before a meeting, seminar or networking event. Dental floss is your friend and that bit of apple or spinach really doesn't help you make the best first impression.

3. Body odour: good personal hygiene is essential to create a positive impact. Carry deodorant and keep a couple of clean shirts or blouses in your car to keep you smelling fresh as a daisy, especially during warm weather.

4. Subtle fragrance: an effective personal scent should be like a gentle caress and not a slap in face! A small amount of a light, subtle perfume or aftershave is the best option rather than a heavy, overpowering scent that makes everyone's eyes water!

5. Nasal hair: if your nasal hair is dangling down like a corn field on a windy day then it's time to trim and tidy it away. Excessive nasal fuzz can be distracting and unsightly. A little extra attention to personal care can make a huge difference."

Learn more from Tristan and connect with him on social media via his website tristanlee.com

Open networking

Where you are attending networking events that are specifically 'open networking' events, or simply have a part of the session where you have the chance to roam around without a formal structure, I would recommend you avoid becoming part of a regular clique. It can be intimidating to guests and off-putting to existing members when they see the same group of people standing together in the same place each time. The appearance of an 'old boys' club' certainly won't serve you. So, whilst it is great to build relationships with those people who are also part of that clique, it is important not to do so to the detriment of making other connections.

Always attempt to keep an open circle when you are standing with others in a group, rather than a closed huddle. Even if others don't join you, they don't want to be left with a bad taste having been shut out.

One way I tried to be different to others was to use the open networking session not just to speak to those who have already referred me or become my customer, but to attempt to break the ice with those who have appeared a little withdrawn, nervous, shy or indeed those who I think may be trying to avoid me. Where I needed to break down barriers, I would be sure to not only ask lots of questions about that person's business and the ideal referrals they were looking for, but also to really try and get to know them and find out about what they like to do in their spare time, their family and the holidays they enjoy taking. How many other parts of our relationship-building activities could this apply to?

How to open and close your introductions

In the formal introductions part of any networking meeting, often referred to as the 60 seconds round, or 40 seconds round, the way you start and finish your introduction will help people to remember who you are and what you do.

I strongly recommend network marketers to clearly introduce themselves as representatives of their chosen company, and not try to hide behind words which don't give it away. It is an immediate erosion of the trust you are trying to build with the people around you if you are evasive or embarrassed about who you partner with.

To put it another, and possibly harsher, way. If you're embarrassed about the company you represent, to the extent that you try to conceal it - why on earth are you with them?

Stand up, state clearly who you are and who you represent and then, at the end of your introduction, repeat the same.

This is one area which doesn't carry over in every part of your other prospecting approaches. For example, we would recommend avoiding screaming company names on social media, to avoid turning it into what Wes would call 'anti-social media'. Subtle is a better approach on social media, likewise at the Christmas dinner table!

Wearing more than one hat

Genuinely, network marketers do have some work to do to build up credibility in their networking and social groups. This isn't your fault, but it's what you need to contend with based on some untrained, hunter mentalities. It's fine, though, if you follow the advice in this book you can become one of the most valued and referred people in your group. However, you have to set the odds in your favour... I seriously advise you pick your horse and ride it - and then keep riding it. People are more likely to buy into the idea of referring someone they believe to be serious about their business, and whilst they will appreciate you may also have a job or conventional business that is your bread and butter work, I feel you'll lose any hope of credibility if you start promoting lots of opportunities at the same time:

"Hello everyone, my name is Jim and if your skin is feeling a bit saggy, I represent the 'Always Young' company and can provide you with our magic cream to help you look twenty years younger. If you're feeling overweight, you must try my weight-loss shakes from 'Skinnylives' and if you want to save money on

your electricity then I am partnered with 'The Discount Centre'. And if your tin opener never opens tins properly then I have my 'HomeEssentials' catalogue with me; and finally, I also now have an online-only opportunity where you buy some trading chips and hopefully they'll be worth 563,824,879 times more in a year, so refer me to everyone you know, for basically everything you can think of..."

Let's just imagine that you are in the room and the plumber stands up and says he can fix laptops, get you a conservatory, install blinds, teach your kids to drive and landscape your garden, as well as hypnotise you out of your smoking habit - what would you think? Would you take him seriously as a professional in his space who you can trust to focus on your referral? Or would you see him as a 'Jack of all trades' who isn't focused?

I'm all for multiple streams of income but I would advise you to think carefully about how you will appear to the group if you seem to be riding several horses. If you want to be seen as someone who is seriously committed to their network marketing business, then you just avoid the temptation to represent several network marketing businesses. Quite aside from the fact that people won't take you seriously, I cannot think of anyone who has successfully built a team in more than one business at the same time. You may generate some pocket money from this approach but if you're looking to build a strong, long-term, residual income and be taken seriously in your networking circles, you'll be well advised to ride just the one horse.

Finding customers or building a team?

It's worth remembering that some networking groups will only allow you to promote the retail side of your business. In my personal opinion, it never sounds or feels right at networking groups when you start trying to pitch the making money, business opportunity side of your business. I feel you have to be particularly skilled to explain the income proposal of any network marketing business in 40 to 60 seconds.

Indeed, even if you have one of the extended four, five or ten minute presentation slots, I still generally feel you are likely to struggle to impress your audience and you'll end up seeing some folded arms and huffing! I believe success in network marketing comes from eyeball-to-eyeball interactions, and it may well be that there are people in your group who will find the idea of becoming a distributor with your company an appealing one, alongside their current business. However, if they have been party to some negative comments about 'pyramids' after witnessing less than successful attempts to explain how the money works in a group setting, they will probably think again. When you have a one-to-one with fellow members you get the chance to explain how your business works, but once again, I would show them purely from a perspective that they know how best to refer you rather than so you can ask, *"So when are you joining?"*.

In my opinion, providing it doesn't breach the rules of the group, you could occasionally - and I mean occasionally - spotlight the profile of a person who you have recently introduced to your business. I would be quite specific with the story, however, and explain that you are looking for referrals to people like them, with similar backgrounds or priorities.

The approach I would absolutely avoid like the plague is the *'I'm looking for absolutely anyone - if you eat, drink, sleep or breathe, this business is for you'* approach. It's crass, and however true you may believe it to be, people in networking groups have seen and heard (and rejected) this line many times before you said it! This would be the same in all your prospecting endeavours, no matter how great you believe your business to be.

In conclusion, prepare yourself well, and be conscious of how you're presenting yourself, and you have every chance of making a great impression at these events. Furthermore, these pointers should help you in the other environments you are prospecting in.

Chapter 4

How to promote specific business types at networking events

Wes Linden

Attending networking events can be an excellent gateway for growing your network marketing business - even in your spare time - but it is vital you take it as seriously as the most serious person there.

Why? Well, whether we like it or not, there will be people that have prejudged you as soon as they know you're in network marketing and it is your job to show them that you are serious and professional, and to prove that you can be as valuable a member as anybody else.

Don't get hung up on the prejudging thing. If we are honest, even when we try not to, we all prejudge a little and there will be estate agents, independent financial advisers, accountants, car dealers, life coaches and no end of other professionals who will have to overcome some prejudice in a networking environment. They may prove to be fantastic at what they do, and we just need to do the same too.

I actually preferred going into networking groups where they had a negative view of my company or the profession, because it gave me a chance to surprise and delight people. I often likened it to going into a new relationship - if all your new partner does is rave about their ex, you may find it harder to make a positive impact, whereas if they've not had a hugely cheery array of previous encounters, it may prove simpler to make a great impression!

Let's consider some of the different types of network marketing businesses that you could be in, and how you can stand out:

Weight loss

I'm not going to be as crass as to suggest that an overweight person cannot promote weight loss, but if you are perhaps not at your curvy best (girls) or looking lean and trim (guys), then you will need to ensure you are very clearly on that weight loss journey. This means ensuring that if you go to a breakfast networking group, you don't fill your plate with a full, greasy English fry-up! People will be watching you - and seeing you buttering several slices of white toast to dip into your fried eggs is certainly going to get people talking.

So, fruit salad it is then! Alongside of course, the weight loss shake that you promote.

If you are on that journey yourself, and you are clearly 'living it', this is likely to be a great conversation starter. I would urge you to relax with it though and not become a bore to those you are sitting around by criticising their choice of bacon and sausages. I've witnessed this approach before and it generally irritates people.

I would also consider creating your own folder with transparent pouches, where you can insert testimonial letters along with before and after pictures, including your own. Whilst this content may be presented on your social media pages, I am a believer in making it as easy as possible to help people recommend you, and having this with you, so you can share examples with those who are interested, and use them in your one-to-ones too.

Finally, I believe it's really bad practice to criticise other businesses in a similar sector to you. However, with something as emotionally-charged as weight loss, you can do some irreparable damage by criticising the path that someone is already on. It's very easy to do with a throwaway comment, but if, for example, someone in your group mentions that they are using a different type of shake, a specific exercise regime, or attending a weekly slimming club, I would recommend you avoid the temptation to jump in with some negative feedback or well-meaning advice on why their choice is a dreadful one - even if it is!

Instead, it may be better to say, *"Great! And how has that been going for you?"*

At least then you have an idea of where they are at on their journey, rather than getting their back up. Remember also, you're looking for referrals, and not necessarily for every member to become a customer of yours. Almost everybody could say they know some other people who have had several failed attempts at weight loss, and clearly not every method suits each individual. So, work with your members to get introductions to those people, rather than trying to sell all of them into your programme, whether they need to lose weight or not!

Health, wellness and beauty

My advice here for people in health and wellness is pretty similar to that above for those offering weight loss products, as well as other healthy alternatives to coffee and chocolate. Firstly, you need to look the part. Whether you look like Posh or Becks isn't the issue, but it's important you look like you're working towards vitality both inside and out.

This may mean waking up early enough to make sure you look fresh and vibrant, because if the only time your networking colleagues see you is between seven and nine in the morning, and you are looking half-asleep and not at your best, then I have some bad news. However good your content is, however good your relationship-building skills are, however good your products are, many people are going to judge you on their first impression, which is that you aren't walking your talk. This is the same if you are trying to promote your products to the other parents at the school gates, for example.

The following advice is true for everyone, but even more so for you! You should be sure to have some fresh breath spray or chewing gum, and try to avoid coffee, curry or cigarette aromas!

As with those in weight loss, a before and after photos folder will be good, but of course, some of your strongest testimonials will be about how people feel inside, so be sure to get lots of endorsement letters and emails printed out and filed into your folder too.

Again, avoid the temptation to criticise what people are currently doing. My experience with many companies in the health, wellness and beauty industries is that they offer some incredible products that achieve far greater results than the stuff that is advertised to us day in, day out. However, advertising creates strong subconscious bonds due to the celebrity endorsements, the music, the colours, the subliminal messages we get, so mocking or knocking someone's choice or preference will likely lead to disengagement.

Use open questions to find out what people look for in a product. For example, *"Do you make your buying decisions based on cost or quality?"*, and when you're told the type of product a person uses, perhaps ask, *"Is this the first time you have used it, or is it something you have regularly used?"*

Once they answer you may probe further with a question like, *"So is it results, habit or advertising that keeps you going back to that product?"*

I would urge that you do not see each person in your group as a potential customer but instead as someone who can introduce you to an unlimited number of potential customers. If you get a reputation in your group for being someone who is always trying to push your products to the other members, you'll lose their goodwill when it comes to them recommending you.

Utility services & membership clubs

For those in networks that promote utility services or the benefits of a members' club, you may well be thinking that an advantage you have is that the services or club benefits you can offer are often everyday consumables. This could work in your favour but you may also find it works against you sometimes, because there will be fellow members who have sought out a 'deal' for themselves in the past, or are contracted to suppliers, or have particular favourite companies they have a loyalty towards.

However strange you may find those loyalties or deals, it is vital that you don't express exasperation towards your fellow members at their decisions. Remember, they're your referral team, they don't actually *have* to be your customer (even though they may be in the future).

When you can offer tangible benefits, better service and decent savings for your potential customers, you really need to find a way to show this in your 40/60 seconds. I wouldn't be quoting rates and tariffs – after all, most people don't know what they're paying to start with anyway. Don't make it about price - even if you're £1 per month cheaper here or 50 cents cheaper somewhere else, this should be considered insignificant compared to the value and benefits they will be getting by using your service. If you bring it down to just pennies and dimes, you are neglecting the personal touch and value that they will get by giving their custom to you. Here's a great quote you should keep in mind - *'People don't buy the plane, they buy the destination'.*

Of course, there will be occasions where you have a big headline story that sounds impressive and is verifiable (rather than marketing hype), and you may wish to lean on this occasionally. This will also appeal to the bean counters in the room. I would urge you to be sporadic with this though - for example, if you can demonstrably state that your company is doing a promotion where, for example, they will save £300 per year on a particular utility compared to all the other providers, then there's benefit to mentioning this. However, I would remind you that by shouting about prices all the time, you are focusing on the plane and not the destination, and, significantly, you will shift people to focus purely on price when they deal with you.

Greetings cards

Those involved with businesses who offer greetings cards look as to how they can stand out, and should have an ideal opportunity to do so. Greetings cards seem to fall into one of four categories as I see it right now:

1) the expensive cards from certain well-established high street stores, as well as upmarket boutique shops;

2) the cheaper cards of lower quality from the newer high street stores and budget shops;

3) the cards that are ordered easily online and can be personalised with photos and messages;

4) the panic purchases made in petrol stations or local convenience stores when you realise you have been forgetful!

Those who generally shop at the more expensive stores are likely to choose to do so based on quality, whereas those who use the cheaper outlets are likely to be mindful of price. Those who order online may well be looking for convenience as well as the chance to be extra thoughtful with personalisation. We have all probably fallen into category four at some time or another, but it's almost certainly not the position of choice!

When you deliver your 40 or 60 second pitch you should look to address these different categories, although not all at once. I would always recommend you cover one point well, highlighting what makes you stand out ahead of one of the tried and tested preferences listed above, and make it very clear who your ideal, targeted referral is each week, rather than try and tick every box each time you stand up to speak.

Expecting people to change habits is not easy, but done thoughtfully, where the pleasure of the benefits outweigh the pain of change, and you could find yourself with a regular supply of referrals.

With this particular niche, you are well-poised to demonstrate and show real examples of what products you can offer and how they stand out.

Household items

Where you have a business that provides essential household items, which might often be promoted via catalogues, you have a platform to reach an entirely different audience than you would on your door-to-door rounds. Stefan confirms to me that he rarely sees people from household catalogue businesses on the networking circuit and we both agree that this is a shame - for those prepared to take their business a little bit more seriously, we believe you could not only make a good return from networking, but also be a really important contributor to your group due to the numbers of people you get to interact with on your rounds.

Your business is easy to understand and you can offer a personal delivery service (either during the week or at the meeting) that removes the hassle of missed deliveries when ordering online, or town centre trips and parking. This is, of course, a convenience for fellow members, but you should work hard to emphasise the benefits of shopping with you for all the people they know.

Where you have niche products, this is obviously something you can play on and demonstrate. Additionally, where the quality of your product shines over what most people would have bought from the traditional stores, you can most certainly show this during your 40 or 60 second introduction.

It is fairly difficult to try and directly compete with what companies like Amazon do well so I would most certainly play on the convenience and personal touch that you can bring to the table.

In all cases I would advise leaning on testimonials and stories about other relatable scenarios – providing you don't waffle or overdo the details, you can regularly share a story of someone, or a couple, who you have helped in the previous couple of weeks. I always believe that the best way to tell a story is to tell it like a story – so share their name to give them an identity, touch on how you know them and what they do, what generation they are and how you helped them.

For example (include your standard introduction and close):

"This week I went to see Martin and Caroline, who run a printing business in town. They're in their late forties and things are tight for them and when we were chatting they mentioned that it's rare for them to get a night out. So, I was able to introduce them to our discount house and save them around £45 per month on things they were paying for already, and ensure they never have to experience bad service from faceless suppliers again. The best

bit? They said that this means they can have a date night each month with the money they've saved. This week, I would love you to think about people you know who perhaps work hard, and are perhaps like ships in the night, who I could help to have a date night each month without them doing anything differently."

Or...

"Thanks to Bev in this group, I got to meet her friend, Mandy, last month, who was fed up with yo-yo dieting. We put her on our Fab 14 plan and worked on a nutritional timetable that suited her lifestyle. She's lost a healthy three kilos over the past four weeks, and has committed to another two months because she wants to feel confident in her bikini this summer instead of feeling embarrassed. So, today I'm asking you to think about people you know who have regularly been attempting to diet but never succeeded in losing weight, as people who you could refer me to."

I am a big fan of creating 40 and 60 second introductions with real names, people and stories involved, and where you can share relatable and real, good news examples. If you can also indicate that someone was a referral from someone else in the chapter, you will really score, as you are indirectly crediting the referrer, whilst indicating clearly that it is okay to refer you because others in the group are.

Finally, do consider the importance of varying your introductions and not only making them story-based, as different personality types will appreciate alternate styles, as described in Chapter 6.

Be the network marketer that you would like to deal with, and make the effort to think through and plan your approaches, and with the long game in mind, I'm confident you can prosper.

Chapter 5

Diff'rent Strokes - how to approach different types of networking events

Stefan Thomas

A long time ago, in a chapter far, far away... sorry, I'm a *Star Wars* fan!

Anyway, back in Chapter 1, we talked about the different networking organisations which exist and, in Chapter 4, we talked about how to promote different types of businesses at networking events.

This chapter could set you head and shoulders above any competition you may have because it covers something which so many people fail to understand.

Just because something is called 'a networking event', it doesn't mean that it is the same as the other networking event you went to last week. Just because you meet some people over breakfast and stand up and introduce your business to them, it doesn't mean that you should say the same thing at every single event.

I meet a lot of people at networking events every week and sometimes I come across a huge amount of frustration.

People tell me, very regularly, that they are really frustrated because they've been very successful in one networking group, but they've then joined another and it just doesn't work as well for them.

There can be loads of reasons why this is the case. But one reason which comes up time and again is that people are attempting to use the same approach everywhere because, after all, it's networking, right? It's all the same, surely?

It is incredibly important to work out the structure and culture of each networking group, and then adjust your approach accordingly. It is ***MUCH*** easier to simply do the same thing everywhere and, as with an awful lot of business marketing, the opportunity lies in the fact that most people won't bother to change their approach, so those that do will stand out.

So, something important to work out even before you attend, is what sort of networking event you are going to, what the structure is, whether there is an introduction (40 or 60 seconds) round and what you should be trying to achieve if there is.

You will usually know who is organising the networking event if you booked directly, or who invited you if that is how you ended up there. I would put the time into asking in advance what you should expect and what format the networking will take.

In my experience, the format and structure of the meeting tends to fall into one of the following types:

Open/unstructured networking

This is the sort of event where you literally pitch up into a room full of people and make conversation. Very often this is the type of networking which happens before some sort of event such as a corporate presentation. Often, a new business will have a launch event or something similar and advertise 'networking' as part of the deal. I recall a time where a local accountancy firm would invite me to an event every year to explain the budget and one of the attractions was the 'networking' which accompanied the event. This wasn't networking in the same way as BNI, 4Networking, Athena or others with any sort of structure, just simply an opportunity to meet other local businesses. No less valuable for that, but without any of the expectations that you needed to have anything prepared.

For open events, instead of a formal 40 or 60 second introduction, you only have to think about how you are going to open conversations with people. Remember that the networking event is only the start of the conversation. All you need to do is get chatting. I always set the bar very low by talking about the presentation, the parking, the location of the tea, coffee or loos, the food, or to be very British about it, the weather! Don't overthink this at all, get chatting and during the conversation the other party will always ask, *"So, what do you do?"*, at which point you have the chance to introduce yourself and swap cards.

Structured/formal networking

In describing this type of networking as 'formal' I don't mean you have to wear your Sunday best, or even that there are a ton of rules. I simply mean there is some sort of format to help to make the event, and the meeting, flow. There are plenty of different formats which I will try to describe below, but the difference between this sort of event and the one described above is that the meeting, and you, will stick to a preset format from beginning to end. The format, to a degree, dictates how you approach the meeting and how you introduce yourself in the formal introductions round.

One important difference is that often the start and end times at unstructured events are guidelines - often people turn up halfway through the event as there is no set format. At structured events it is really important to be there on time and plan to be there at least until the end (see Chapter 2) as you will miss out on some of the format if you do not.

Networking vs referral marketing

This is where it gets interesting, as even what we describe generically as 'networking' might actually be something subtly different, and this is where people very often get tripped up.

This is my best attempt at describing the differences.

Networking is an opportunity to start conversations, to build relationships and to get to know people to the extent where they trust you to either do business with you directly, or refer business to you.

Referral marketing is an opportunity to educate other business owners in not only what you do, but what type of clients or customers you are looking for, with a joint understanding that you will actively look for business opportunities (referrals) for each other.

Most membership networking organisations fit into one or the other category. BNI, for example, are a referral marketing organisation ('The World's Biggest Referral Marketing Organisation') where 4Networking, for example, are a networking organisation (and describe themselves as 'The UK's Only Joined Up Business Network').

To make it even more confusing, the two types of events are often very similar in their structure. Taking the breakfast meetings on their own, both BNI and 4Networking have open networking at the beginning, followed by a scripted, formal part of the meeting which includes both an introduction (40 or 60 seconds) round at both, and a presentation from a member.

Superficially, therefore, it would be easy to imagine that you could turn up at each one and do exactly the same. After all, you eat breakfast and stand up and speak for about a minute, so it's the same, isn't it?

Many networking events (in the UK at least) follow a very similar structure to either 4Networking or BNI, so I shall concentrate mainly on them.

At BNI, the point of your 60 second introduction is to educate the other attendees as to what your business does and what type of referral you are looking for. The more specific the better, as specificity helps the other people in the room to picture which of their contacts they should refer to you. The introduction is then backed up by BNI's culture and stated expectation of members actively looking for referrals for each other, as well as the structure of the meeting which has a section for referrals to be passed.

Specifically, your call to action at a BNI meeting should be to be entirely clear on exactly what referrals you are looking for. Specificity works because if you tell people you are simply looking for anyone with a house, that is too big a group of people for them to think of. If you tell them you are looking for people who own a three-bedroomed semi in a specific cul-de-sac in a specific village, it helps them to completely understand who you are looking for, and may even prompt the one person in the room who knows exactly that person. Being clear, incidentally, on your ideal client, is really important in any business and could really help you here.

The 40 second introduction at a 4Networking meeting should, in my opinion, be used purely to encourage the others in the room to want to have a one-to-one with you. You aren't immediately canvassing for referrals, you are giving people enough information about your business to entice them to want to find out more. The 4Networking meeting structure has three rounds of ten minute one-to-ones as part of the meeting. Your 40 seconds is your advert to get people queuing for a one-to-one with you.

Help people to understand the outcome of working with you. What will they end up with, how will they feel, what have other clients and customers said about you? To put it simply, why should someone ask you for a one-to-one and give up 10 minutes of their life to spend talking to you?

Aside from the introductions round, there are other differences between the 4Networking and BNI structure which are vitally important to understand.

At BNI, the 10 minute member presentation is specifically for that member to talk further about their business in detail and the type of referrals they are looking for. At 4Networking the 4Sight presentation is for a member to give a presentation and specifically not a sales pitch. Once again, the differences are subtle but really important. Once again, an area where one size definitely does not fit all.

Also, the expression 'one-to-one' is used at both organisations, but means subtly different things. In 4Networking the one-to-one is something which happens within the meeting and is a 10 minute opportunity for two attendees to get to know each other better. At BNI the one-to-one is something which each member is encouraged to organise with each other member outside of the meeting, in a specific meeting to get to know each other, and what type of referrals each is looking for.

Other types of networking format which exist and you may be invited to include:

Speed networking

Fast, furious and noisy. Broadly speaking, the attendees sit in two lines facing each other. Each is typically given one minute to talk to the other and after that time the lines shift so you get a new person to talk to.

Big tip for speed networking - resist the opportunity to talk about yourself. Ask about the other person, ask for their contact details and, crucially, ask their permission to call them after the event for a slightly less frenetic opportunity to chat. And then do it!

Co-working

Typically, the domain of creatives and facilitated by various organisations who own co-working spaces across the world. As a network marketing professional, you are less likely to find yourself at a specific co-working event, but if you do, they are basically open networking events, but held in a space where people are working. Typically, as part of the session, there is a round table or similar session where you get to interact with the others.

Mastermind/support groups

Some networking organisations offer specific 'closed' sessions where the attendees share their current business challenges and attempt to help each other work through them. This is a massive opportunity for you if you have experience or skills which might help other people. The opportunity is to show yourself as a rounded and selfless business person.

Summary

Don't ever forget, and I'm unlikely to let you, that the networking event is the start of the conversation. Find out which type of networking event you are going to, either by speaking to people in advance, or, and just as usefully, pitching up the first time and sussing it out. Then stand out by crafting your approach specifically for that event and its culture and people, instead of lazily just rolling out the same thing you do every week at every other event. The effort is not to be ignored, but the potential returns are huge, the real opportunity being, of course, that most people won't bother.

Chapter 6

Going beyond the basics - how to make even more of an impact at networking events

Wes Linden

"I can't wait to get to my networking group this morning to be sold to!"

I love Stefan's philosophies on how everybody goes to networking for the sake of their own business. My networking philosophy was always to have a deep understanding of this, and to zig whilst everyone else zagged. So, I put my mindset in a place that I was simply going to my networking groups to serve them and to find ways to support their businesses. How true this is also for other ways of prospecting, whereby you become known as a supportive and helpful person, rather than someone trying to sell stock.

By taking this approach, I would reckon that long-term I was always one of the busiest receivers of referrals in the group. Strange that - by selflessly looking to be a great referrer, long-term, I ended up gaining lots and lots of referrals.

In effect, I made myself the most referable person in the room by serving others. This is why I like the idea that we can 'win the room' rather than 'work the room'.

In this chapter, I will share some tips to help you think outside the box so you can operate with a 'give first, get later' approach.

Going the extra mile

Every time you use the service of another member, be sure to do a complimentary post on social media sharing how impressed you were with them and their service. Where possible, get a photo with them to personalise it, or a picture of them at work. If it's possible in your networking group, also share praise during the meeting itself.

You'll not only get more referrals for people doing this from your social media network, but you'll find people *want* to be referred by you because they know you'll work hard to amplify their service. And if they want to be referred by you, how could they best build that relationship with you than by working hard to find you referrals!

There's no reason this shouldn't work in day-to-day life too, whether you ever go to a single networking group or not. So many people want to use social media to complain about a rude waiter, or to moan about the queue at the dentist, why not be an amplifier of good news and good service, and let the bad experiences wash over you rather than sharing them?

Furthermore, try and keep your radar on at all times. So, for example, if someone you know says they're looking to sell their house, be sure to check with them if they need a solicitor, or a mortgage broker for their new purchase, or a gardener to ensure their garden looks good for the photos, or a cleaner to do a deep-clean prior to viewings? Or an electrician, plumber or decorator for when they buy their new place? If someone has bought a new car, do they need a mobile valet to keep it looking great, or an insurance broker for the personal touch? If someone is having a party, do they need a DJ, a live band, a magician, a party planner, party bags, costume hire, a hairdresser or make-up artist, party novelties? Do they need invites printed, cakes made, catering provided? There's a myriad of chances for you to support members of your networking groups, by making the effort and thinking outside the box.

This works brilliantly even if you aren't doing business networking, to become a connector of people - someone who makes friends and helps their friends - will make you a 'go to' guy or gal, which makes you far more likely to have people wanting to do business with you.

There's no end of opportunities to find referrals that possibly wouldn't end up at your door if you don't think of asking these questions. But think of the difference it would make if you do.

Being part of the networking management team

Another way to increase your visibility is to find a role you would want to fulfill within the group. When you are sitting at the head of the table, or you're involved in organising aspects of the meeting, it is human nature that you're going to be a person that people want to stretch themselves to help and support. You'll also be one of the more prevalent faces seen by visitors and new members.

Most of these roles are only for 6 to 12 months but you can gain an awful lot of kudos and credibility in that time. Naturally, people are also more motivated to help someone they see as a committed member who is putting themselves out, rather than those who sit on the periphery.

Getting visitors to your networking events

Experience taught me that working hard to find visitors for the group was also very good for building up goodwill within the group. Whether it was calling or texting local business owners, speaking to people I came into contact with during the course of my week, or watching local Facebook groups and reaching out to people who were running small businesses, I found that putting this extra effort in really did increase my influence in the group. Naturally, if the person saw value in joining the group, they would be grateful to you for the introduction and you're likely to find they'll work hard to repay you by referring you.

Understanding that contacts aren't prospects, yet

People don't go to networking events to be your prospects - and sometimes that confuses people. A networking meeting isn't the same as a sales meeting. If you called a potential customer and organised to go and meet them, they would expect to be your prospect, they would know exactly the purpose of the meeting - that you were going to be introducing your products or services to them, and, presumably, that you might ask them to buy.

But a networking meeting is different. Everyone is there for their own reasons but, and without interviewing everyone attending the same meetings as you, I can be reasonably sure that they went to promote their business, or receive the support and friendship of their networking colleagues. They didn't get up at 5am with the intention of being your prospects, or subjecting themselves to being *'sold to'*.

No different to Friday night in the pub or the school's Sports Day, the reason for being with the people there is not for them to be sold to - it doesn't mean conversations can't happen there which lead to opportunities, but you probably need to leave the sandwich board at home.

Now here's the thing, that doesn't mean that these guys won't buy from you, it doesn't mean that some of them won't turn into your prospects. It means that you will get better results, ultimately, by respecting why other people attend networking events, having some patience, and allowing the relationships to flourish before suggesting to the right people that they might be interested in working with you or buying from you.

Understanding and communicating with different personality types

One of the phrases we often hear is that you should be yourself. This is certainly something I subscribe to, as you'll appear fairly transparent if you are always trying to be someone you're not. However, one skill every networker should have is an understanding of how best to interact with different personality types.

If you have someone who loves the parties and social interaction, there's no point focusing on the minutiae and fine tooth-comb details of your product or business, whereas if you have someone who is ultra-analytical and introverted, there's little point in telling them about the fun side of joining your business, or the monthly customer appreciation parties you have where you all get together and socialise.

The network marketing legend Tom 'Big Al' Schreiter wrote a terrific book on understanding the personality types called *'The Four Color Personalities for MLM: The Secret Language for Network Marketing'*. I would recommend you get a copy.

How to respond to the referrals you get

It always astonishes me when I give someone a referral and they message me to say, *"I have sent an email"*, or *"I sent them my website link"* or *"I have dropped them a text"* about the person I have referred them to. **What???!!!**

If local networking is about the personal touch, how are you going to create the magic KLT - Know, Like, Trust? It'll simply be DKDLDT. This stands for 'Don't Know, Don't Like, Don't Trust'! When you have a personal recommendation from someone, you actually have a really great chance to change the KLT to 'Know, Love, Trust', but you'll never have that if you're hiding behind a keyboard.

So, when you get a referral, my advice is to ensure you are contacting them on the phone by *calling* them, within 24 hours. The longer you leave it, the colder it gets. You want them to be saying, *"Wow, that's quick, we were only speaking about you yesterday"*, rather than struggling to remember why it is they wanted a call from you.

Obviously, if you fail to get hold of them, my advice would be to leave them a courtesy message to let them know you have been in touch and back it up with a text. However, do not assume they'll ring you back, even if you ask them to. People are busy and there's a good chance that becoming your customer is not the only thing they have to do that day! However, that doesn't mean you shouldn't try again a day or two later, just as with any prospecting approach, it will require you to be proactive rather than taking offence if someone doesn't call you back.

How to actively ask for referrals

'For every one that asketh receiveth; and he that seeketh findeth; and to him that knocketh it shall be opened.' Matthew 7:8

Wouldn't it be great if it were really that easy, that you just needed to ask and you would get exactly the referrals you wanted?

Matthew, of course, wasn't writing about referrals when he wrote the above passage, well, not as far as we know at least. But too many people try to attract referrals without ever asking, and that is completely doomed to failure.

Before you ask your networking buddies for referrals, make sure you're absolutely clear on who you want to be referred to. Be specific, even down to the actual person you want to speak to.

Vague criteria such as *"I'm looking for anyone with a house",* or *"I'd like to speak to anyone who wants to improve their health"*, simply won't work. They put the responsibility of thinking about the referral onto the person you want the referral from. Instead of making them have to think about who to refer to you, on top of all of the more pressing matters they have to think about, make it easy for them by being really, forensically, specific. If that means doing some research, then do it and don't expect another busy business owner to do it for you.

But ask. If you're a member of a networking group which encourages members to refer business to each other, then people are expecting to be asked and you will increase your chance of receiving referrals by several hundred percent if you start asking people.

There is a way of simultaneously and hugely increasing the number of referrals you receive whilst making it super easy to ask people. And that is to look for referrals for them. When it comes to the part of the meeting when people explain the type of referral they are looking for, don't look down and presume you can't help. Listen, get a notebook and make notes, and then spend part of your working week actively seeking referrals for others in the room. The simplest way that I've found to do that, if you don't personally know the person who your networking buddy wants to speak to, is to listen to who other people want to meet, then pick up the phone and invite them to your networking meeting. Whenever you're successful, pick up the phone to the person who wanted to meet that person to a) ensure they'll be there, and b) enjoy them thanking you and asking if there is anything they can do for you.

Win-win, as they say.

And who knows, the person you invited to the networking group may well end up grateful to you that you invited them. That has happened to me more times than I care to count.

Pulling it together

You'll have noticed a theme in this book so far. Networking works, if you do it right. It works if you're thoughtful and do things properly and go the extra mile, ensuring you do what others aren't prepared to. If you zig when everyone else zags, and do it consistently, you'll get the results that others can only hope for.

Chapter 7

Farming not hunting - building a long-term valued profile

Wes Linden

If you have spent any time around networking events so far, you may well have heard these two common terms - 'hunter' and 'farmer'.

Being known as a 'hunter' is absolutely not a badge of honour. This term isn't just reserved for network marketers by any stretch of the imagination. It can be used to describe anyone who arrives at a networking group for a couple of the free taster weeks, charges around the group doing what is termed 'working the room'; throwing business cards at anybody who moves, adding everyone to their email list and spamming them with sales messages, spending no time getting to know people or finding out about their businesses, and simply attempting a quick landgrab, before moving on to the next group.

I've seen people from all vocations who have attempted this approach, and savvy networkers can spot it a mile off. These people will get literally nothing from this pathway.

Avoid it at all costs - whether it's because money is short or you are impatient, it will not serve you, your business or those who follow you.

The 'farmer' tag is a much more pleasing one. Farmers, by their very nature, take time, trouble and a great deal of effort into cultivating their crops, resulting in a successful harvest. If you are to be successful in business networking, this should be the approach you commit to.

As I always hear Stefan suggest to people - ask yourself this question - when you go to networking, do you go for the sake of your business, or for the sake of everyone else's?

The answer is, ultimately, that you get up early or give up a lunchtime, and pay your attendance fees and maybe a membership cost for the sake of your business. This is the same with all the other members of your group. Here's the trick though - providing you actually understand this, it is very much to your advantage. If you understand and embrace this, and position yourself accordingly, you really can have great success in these environments and find yourself the most referable person in the room.

How to become the most popular person in the room

You need to build a brand as someone who is believable, approachable, trustworthy, honourable and well-valued within the chapter.

Strive to become the best connector in the room, unconditionally. See who you can refer as often as you can. During my most active networking days, I would ask the customers that I was seeing for my business whether there were any local businesses or services they were looking for right now, and explain that I belonged to a local group of tradespeople and business owners and may be able to refer them to someone I trust. This often resulted in people saying, *"Oh I'm looking to change my accountant"*, or *"We need a tiler"*, or *"Do you know anyone who can provide driving lessons for my daughter?"*

Without initially prompting them they would almost certainly not bring this up. Bingo - you have just created a referral out of nowhere! Even if I don't know someone from my group who can help, there's no harm in saying, *"Give me a couple of hours, I think I know someone who will be able to make a great recommendation for you"*. What then happens is I would ask the question of someone who I trust within the group, and give them a chance to connect one of their contacts from outside the group.

Think about the power of this - you have now helped one of your customers by getting them a trusted referral; you have helped someone in your networking group to gain some goodwill from one of their other contacts, and who knows, you may even get a thank you from the person who gets the work, which allows you to extend your circle of influence.

This is what really helps you stand out as a connector. The more you can create these triangles, the more popular you will become in the group. Popularity leads to people wanting to help and support you too - and you didn't need to become a thoroughly irritating and overt salesman in the process!

How social media can help

We regularly see people asking for recommendations now on social media. This is great because it plays into our hands - social media allows us to see when people want a word-of-mouth recommendation. It seems the days are gone of people looking at the Yellow Pages, and Google is so awash with options that this leads more and more people to look for that personal endorsement. This is where you can win!

If you take time to notice, you'll see that people ask for anything from rat-catchers to reliable plumbers; from massage therapists to mortgage brokers; from wedding photographers to window cleaners. We see it amongst our friends and also on local chat forums and groups. Again, why not be the connector who either recommends someone from your networking group if you have one, or tries to find someone reliable from the group who may have a contact who can help?

This is another way where you can really stand out as a strong and positive member of your community, and in turn, people will be looking to refer you wherever possible.

Overcoming the mess that was left behind for you

There are going to be people who represent every occupation unfavourably. I've witnessed all kinds of plumbers, bank managers, letting agents, mechanics, opticians and printers who, in my opinion, did not cover themselves with glory when I saw them operating at networking events, or within their professional environment. They didn't make themselves referable, and if you take ten other experienced networkers, doubtless they would have their own hot-list of a few people they would avoid.

Outside of networking, there are also police officers, bus drivers, priests, doctors, waiting staff, journalists and teachers who fail to represent their professions as well as they should when they are doing their job.

So, unreferable people exist everywhere. Happily, there's also many more referable people to contend with, which makes it all worthwhile.

The same is true in network marketing. There are some wonderful networkers who brilliantly represent their network marketing business in chapters and groups around the world. Honourable, honest, engaged and enthusiastic, and who have a really good name. The aim of this book is to help you become one of them. However, there are some shoddy ones too who have perhaps unknowingly failed to create the right impression and have not done us any favours.

It may not even be their fault. Very few companies train you how to make the best of networking groups, and if an upline leader did not avail themselves successfully of the possibilities that business networking presents, then they may have been unable to offer sound advice on how to network effectively. Maybe I'm overly positive but I believe that nobody is 100% amazing or 100% dreadful at anything - as my good friend Stephan Longworth, author of the book '*Prepare for Take Off in Network Marketing*', often reminds me *'even a broken clock is right twice a day!'*

Sadly though I must warn you, that because of this, and also due to the disproportionate number of network marketers who have appeared to be 'hunters', you may have to work a little bit harder to win trust. This coupled with the propensity that some have to spam anyone who they get an email address for, means there will be some groups where a few members may initially view you with caution, reserving judgement to see whether you have staying power.

Repairing the mess that has been left for you

So how do you overcome the bad reputation that has been left for you, your company and network marketing in general by someone who has left a trail of destruction behind before deserting the group?

Someone who really has hunted; someone who spammed everyone and threw their business cards around like confetti; perhaps someone who promised much and delivered little, who has disappeared from the group, who happened to represent your company, or be from another networking company (but may have still muddied the waters for you by association).

I encountered this situation with a number of groups. I knew what people were thinking. They would initially avoid one-to-one meetings; they would avoid eye contact or they would roll their eyes and say, *"Oh, we had someone from XYZ before - what an idiot!"*

However, I am a believer that time wins out - and that good people get good things provided they are patient. I am also a believer that you can view this situation as a disadvantage or an opportunity.

Personally, I choose to view it as an opportunity.

Firstly, let's put it into perspective. Has everyone had a bad experience at a restaurant or with buying, selling or renting a home that they would rather not repeat, at least once in their life? Almost certainly yes. However, does that mean that people have stopped eating food, or will never buy, sell or rent another property again? Almost certainly not!

So, let us not believe that we are without a chance of rectifying the situation.

Secondly, have you ever had a relationship with someone who appeared to still be in love with their previous partner, or all their friends and family drone on about how great the ex was? It can be a bit draining and you wonder if you'll ever live up to expectations.

If the previous incumbent of your seat in a new networking group achieved legendary status, and all you hear is how wonderful they were, this can also have its frustrations: pressure to be like them rather than yourself, insecurity over whether you'll ever match up, fear that the group may bypass you with their referrals and send them over to the previous member.

A simple mindset shift is to view a destructive, unpopular, previous member as a chance for you to really shine. Yes, it may take a little longer to win trust, but once you do people are likely to be more effusive about you because you have taken them from a negative viewpoint to a positive one.

So, my advice to network marketers going into this situation is to go straight to work on becoming the best connector in the group. Be as engaged as you can be and work hard to avoid any of the traits of a hunter.

Be confident and reassuring to those who observe *"What an idiot"* the previous person was, and tell them, *"Oh dear, I'm sorry you had a less than positive experience, but I guess every profession has someone who will let their colleagues down, wouldn't you agree?"*. Get their buy-in to this being the case.

I would strongly urge you to remain professional and not openly criticise a previous member, or get dragged into bitching about others.

Tell them, *"I can assure you that I will work hard to make sure you'll have a very different impression of me - and I'm guessing you won't hold Jim's manner against me, will you?"*. Again, get their buy-in that they're not going to tar you with the same brush.

But then you need to do your part and become a great member for the group!

When you are doing your first few 40 or 60 seconds talks, I would encourage you to emphasise a few things, whilst people are getting to know you:

"I take my business very seriously and consider myself a professional, so be assured I will look after anyone you recommend me to."

"I'm keen to get to know you all properly and understand how best I can recommend you."

"I plan to become an active part of this community."

You don't need to do all three each time. I would include at least one, if not two of these things on a rotation over the first few sessions, and there's no harm in you repeating yourself (not everyone will hear everything you say first time, and why not show you are serious?). I would do this for the first few sessions in amongst the other things you are saying during your chance to share with the group, and I would do this whether the previous member from your company was the greatest member in the world, or the worst!

Yes, it takes up some of your seconds – however, it makes you more likeable and will attract more people to want to get to know, like and trust you.

Where you attend a networking group that doesn't have a one member per profession rule, and you have other people from your company in attendance, or distributors from network marketing companies in similar industries, I would implore you to remain polite and civil about them at all times, even if someone attempts to criticise them to you. Even if they have been less professional about you! Indeed, I would go out of my way to edify that other person as this is not only a kind way to behave towards others irrespectively, it is also a way to really separate yourself as a professional and someone who rises above the noise.

Conclusion

The real opportunity here, as Stefan always says, is that most people won't bother - and that's where you can win. You can stand out by making an effort to be a great connector. You can stand out for thinking outside the box when it comes to striving to get referrals for others. You can rise above everyone else when you not only tell people you're serious and professional, but you prove it too. You really, really stand out when you focus on building unconditional relationships.

You exceed expectations when you go the extra mile, even if someone in the group is already a customer of the previous member.

Chapter 8

What if you can't find a networking group to suit you - setting up your own

Stefan Thomas

What if you really want to go networking but there isn't a group close to you, or you can't get into any local groups (sometimes there are restrictions on membership)?

A very simple way of building your network quickly, and making yourself extremely visible at the same time, is to set up and run your own networking group - either alongside an existing organisation, or completely on your own.

I've done both myself, I've helped clients of mine to do both and I know the advantages, pitfalls, opportunities and processes necessary to make either option work.

Being part of running a networking group can accelerate your profile and the number of leads you receive, if you handle it correctly, and equally it needs to be considered a medium- to long-term approach. The way to make it work is to approach it from the point of view of the member/attendee and set out to give them massive value. If approached from the point of view of *"How can I sell to these people?"* it is very likely to fall flat on its face. When was the last time you attended a networking event because you wanted to be sold to?

To run a networking group, particularly if you are launching one from scratch, is going to take an amount of effort, particularly at first. For me, the effort was part of building my personal brand and part of the marketing for my business. This wasn't extra effort, just slightly redirected, but still working towards the overall goal.

Working out how to make this an integral part of your business is important, so that you understand why you're doing it, at every stage, even on the days where it feels harder than usual.

Being part of the networking team with an existing organisation

Each of the more widely spread networking organisations - BNI, 4Networking, Athena, BoB and others in the UK - offer voluntary team roles to their members. Effectively, as a member, you volunteer to be part of the team helping to grow a particular group, or possibly even a number of groups.

Typically, these roles aren't rewarded, but in my opinion and experience, the rewards can far outweigh the effort invested.

These networking organisations each have a structure and a system to follow for each role, taking into account their experience and the needs of their brand and their members.

This is a unique opportunity to raise your profile amongst the local members, give you an excuse to contact anyone, give you an opportunity to show off your skills and your work ethic and put you right at the front when it comes to meeting new visitors and members.

Imagine being the 'go to' person in your networking group, the person who people need to contact if they have any questions or need to know something about the group. Imagine also being amongst the most high-profile people in the group and at the regular meetings.

Also, imagine being able to show off to other local members just how connected you are, by making sure the group was well attended and 'buzzy', whilst at the same time having an excuse to contact any business person locally to invite them along and, of course, make them aware of your business at the same time.

Each network has different names for the different roles within the group, but typically there are opportunities for the person who leads the group and reads the script, the person who takes the money and welcomes people to the group each meeting, the person who is responsible for bringing new people to the group, the person who organises the social events, and various other roles too.

In order to apply, one typically needs to be a member of the organisation already, and for there to be a suitable role available. There will be some sort of leadership structure, and every organisation will have someone responsible for finding new team members. If you're unsure, just ask whoever is in charge of that group.

There are some typical commitments (such as attending every meeting) that you should make yourself aware of before going for it, as well as understanding if there are any explicit rewards. Once again, each organisation will have someone locally whose role it is to be able to explain this.

The pros of joining in with an existing organisation are that they already have the systems and structure, and will already know any pitfalls and shortcuts. You accept that you aren't completely in control, however, and have to fulfill your role in line with their brand.

Setting up your own group

This route is potentially more fulfilling, and involves some more effort, not least because you might be a team of one.

Firstly, you have to be absolutely clear what you want your networking group to look like, what the benefits will be for the people who attend, what it is going to cost to run and, therefore, how much you are going to charge attendees, plus how you are going to market your events so that people turn up.

If the area does have several networking groups, you also need to be very clear why yours is different and why people should attend, rather than going to one of the existing and perhaps more established groups.

Getting people to your launch event typically isn't that hard, because people like to check out something new, but ensuring that people continue to attend is where the effort comes in.

Identifying a suitable venue

How do you want your networking event to feel? What do you want people to say about it afterwards? How many people do you expect to come? How will they be travelling to the event? Are you going to provide food?

All of this, and more, needs to be considered when contemplating the right venue for your group.

Asking for recommendations from others helps, and ultimately, actually visiting the venue and talking to the owner or manager about what you need and what they can offer will be necessary. You may need to check out several venues before you find the one which is right for you.

If you intend to serve food, my significant experience would advise you to choose a venue which already serves food at scale. They are much more likely to be able to help you, and deal with any fluctuations in numbers without it being a problem to them, rather than a venue who is ordering in food and potentially staff for you.

What time of day do you want to run your meeting? And what day of the week? Typically, a venue has quiet times and this might work in your favour, particularly if you can organise your meetings on a day when they are quiet. This means their staff will have more time to attend to your needs.

Also, be very clear how and when the venue will need to be paid. If you are collecting money from people as they arrive, is the venue okay to wait until after the event to be paid. And what if fewer people than you expect turn up? Will the venue still want paying for the number you were expecting, or the number who arrived? All of this is well worth working out in advance so you don't have any unexpected surprises.

Getting people to attend

'Build it and they will come' is best not relied on here. You need to work out a marketing plan for your event, just as you would with your business. Who do you want to attend and how are you going to approach them?

Identifying which business owners or which type of people you would like to be there is the start, followed by working out how to make them aware of the event, so as many of them as possible can make it.

I strongly suggest having a booking system in place so that people do commit to the event, rather than just relying on people telling you they are going to arrive. Eventbrite and TicketTailor are two of the most popular such systems and, if people pay up front, at least they have shown some commitment and, equally as importantly, you won't be out of pocket if they don't get there.

There are, as we write this in 2018, plenty of ways to invite people:

Social media - it goes without saying that you will want to shout about your events on Facebook and LinkedIn, as well as on Twitter and Instagram. Carefully written posts, ideally with images to attract people's attention and, crucially, a link for people to book in, need to be regularly placed all over social media, plus people's comments and questions responded to quickly. There may even be groups on Facebook dedicated to your local area who may permit you to advertise your event.

Email marketing - if you have a list and permission to use it, regularly emailing people is extremely effective. Even if you don't have a list at first, building one of the people who have been, or expressed interest in attending your events as you launch, will help to keep up the momentum.

Local press - if you can, get the local press to mention your event. Some local business publications even have a section dedicated to local networking events. If you don't know where to look, find out the editor's phone number and call them and ask.

Websites - there are plenty of websites dedicated to local events. MeetUp.com, Eventbrite.com, NextDoor.co.uk and FindNetworkingEvents.co.uk to name just a few, where you can promote your event.

Leaflets and traditional marketing - passive marketing shouldn't be ignored, and actually dropping leaflets to local business owners or the people you want to attend will definitely have some response.

Calling people to invite them - nothing beats a good old-fashioned phone call. Remember, you're not selling anything, you've got something of value to offer - the opportunity for a local business owner to meet other people who might do business with them. Crucially, if you're going to pick up the phone, if people say they are coming, offer to book them in there and then. Take the initiative whilst they are hot-to-trot, before something else gets in the way!

An important comment on all of this is that it is never about one big thing. Consistent small actions spread over a period of time beat one big push every single time. Constantly have something appearing on people's timelines or in their inbox or in front of them to remind them about the event, that way you have the best chance of catching people at the right moment when they just get on and book in.

Sometimes I have come across people who have decided to make their event free to the attendees, thinking that will increase the likelihood of people attending, only for it to fall flat on its face. Remember that free isn't just about how much it costs in money terms. For a business person particularly, their time is exceptionally valuable and in short supply. For them to give up a few hours to attend your event, they need to be extremely clear on where the value is to them. Make sure any of your marketing focuses on what they will get out of it.

But what's in it for me?

This is probably a good time to remind ourselves why we're doing this. This is long-tail, profile-raising stuff which accelerates the building of your network. Nevertheless, you still need to fulfill the Meet-Like-Know-Trust.

The way to use your networking group to do this is to consistently deliver on what you promised. Get people there, match people up with others you think would be useful to them, introduce people to each other, be the perfect host. Remember that at each step you're delivering value to them, you're also massively speeding up the MLKT process.

You are also building your list of contacts and your network as you go. All you need to do now is keep in touch.

How much effort is involved in running a networking group?

I have been involved in running networking groups for around 11 years. At one point, I was involved in running 5,000 networking meetings a year. People used to constantly comment on the amount of time I was putting into running events and yet, I always looked at it as time I was investing in my own business.

In order for the events to run successfully and to positively reflect on you and your business you do need to put enough effort into making them successful, but if you consider the profile it will give you and the reputation you will build yourself as someone who can organise a great event, which brings value to others, you can see how you're actually using your time twice. You also have the opportunity to invite the people and businesses you want to meet, once again using your time twice.

Chapter 9

Following up and following on

Stefan Thomas

No matter how well you perform at networking events, no matter how well-crafted your 40 or 60 seconds is, or how brilliant you are at hosting your events, your results will be significantly reduced if you don't follow up after the event.

Think of all the brilliant conversations you have at networking events, that service you really liked, that product you thought would be fantastic as a present for someone. Those conversations you were absolutely convinced you were going to act on and do something.

And then you leave the networking event, get to the car park and switch your phone back on. All of a sudden 'real life' rears its head again. An email from your new distributor because things aren't working out for them, a text from your son/daughter on the way to school to say they've forgotten their lunch/rugby boots/maths homework and can you drop it in for them, a voicemail from someone who wants to place an order and it's the last day of the month.

Those brilliant conversations you had only half an hour ago start to slip down your list of priorities. It is suddenly less vital that you buy that product or service, you need to do all this other stuff, plus you only have 40 minutes to get home, get your child's stuff to school and get to a one-to-one.

Within a few hours those conversations are but a niggling memory.

Within a couple of days, you've forgotten them completely and will only remember again when you bump into the same person in a couple of weeks' time.

Guess what? Everyone in the world is just as busy as you. Everyone in the world has the same challenges on their time as you do and has the same capacity to forget the stuff which isn't urgent.

It is, as I've said before, your job to remind people that you exist, not their job to remember you.

So many positive opportunities die, just because people omit to follow up.

And let me suggest why people don't follow up.

You had a brilliant conversation with someone this morning, they were interested in your product, service or opportunity and you told them you would give them a call. Then you leave the networking event, turn your phone on and guess what?

A couple of days later you remember that you said you were going to call them, but now you're embarrassed that you're late doing so, and you put it off again and, in reality, it never happens.

Sound familiar? I know so because I've been there.

Not only has most of my networking success come from what I've done outside the room and after the event but, crucially, I know that when I've worked one-to-one with people and improved their follow-up, their results have gone through the roof. And I'm going to share with you exactly what I share with them.

It is important to keep in touch with everyone you meet at networking. Those piles of business cards have enormous value to your business but only if you use them, and use them correctly.

The first lesson is that people don't go to networking events to be your prospects. I have watched so many otherwise excellent network marketers crash and burn because they make the mistake of treating everyone like a prospect, particularly in the follow-up.

Just because I didn't immediately say *"No"*, doesn't mean I said *"Yes"*. I'm writing this in the heart of England and English people tend to be polite. Just because you had a chat with someone at a networking event and they didn't run away, still doesn't mean you should aggressively push them to join in your first call after the event.

So, a lot of telling you what you shouldn't do, let's look at what does work.

Active and passive following up - and knowing the difference

I believe there are two types of following up we should all undertake, if we want the maximum success from our networking efforts.

I describe them as active and passive follow up.

Active being the act of following up with someone who has expressed real, genuine, active interest in our product, service or opportunity. We owe it to ourselves, our business, our families and our credit card company to follow that lead up in a timely and professional manner.

Secondly, passive follow-up is everyone else. Those people who we just chatted to, where there was no immediate interest on either side. In my opinion and experience it is even more valuable to keep in touch with this group of people over a period of time. My experience, incidentally, is that, ultimately, more business has come from this group of people. Not immediately, but over time the difference has been huge.

I promise you, and you can message me on social media when it comes true, that keeping in touch with the people you meet, at scale, will make a huge difference to your business over time.

So, breaking the two down.

Actively following up

Let's look first at how you know someone is interested. As above, it isn't just because they don't immediately say *"No"*, it's important to be able to spot some buying signals and act on them.

In my first job, in 1983, I was taught how to spot buying signals and how to act on them. As I mentioned earlier, I worked in the gent's department of a shoe shop and tell-tale signs were when someone held the same shoe for a while, or started to try one on, or stood gazing longingly at a particular shoe. Alternatively, the person might ask you if you had that shoe in their size, or a different colour (this was the gent's department and it was 1983, so you got black, very dark grey, or brown if you were a dangerous rule breaker).

Once you spotted any of these signs, you would approach the person and say, *"How can I help, Sir?"*. Note the open question by the way.

Things aren't quite so simple these days. Those buying signals are more likely to come up in conversation and are likely to be more subtle. In fact, a lot of buying signals come as apparent challenges or objections.

Sometimes, just sometimes, during a networking one-to-one, someone will say, *"That's great, where do I sign?"*, or *"Can I buy a six month supply"*, or *"Is it okay if 18 of my friends join too?"* I hope you don't need me to tell you that those are buying signals. They are also signals to open the wine/Prosecco/soft drink of your choice that evening.

But a lot of buying signals look a bit like this:

"It looks great but I'm not sure I'd have the time."

"I really love it, but isn't it quite expensive?"

"This sounds brilliant, but I'm already in a contract."

"I would need to check with my wife/husband/partner first."

In this situation, it is your role to take the lead in what happens next. This means moving the conversation forward positively which, if I were sat there, would sound a bit like this:

"Do you know, so many people initially think they don't have the time, and pretty much everyone successful in the business thought that at first. Have you got 20 minutes tomorrow when we can actually look at it and work out if you do?"

"I've heard that many times before, but you know what, it probably works out less expensive in the long run than what you're already using. Any chance I can pop round and show you how that's worked out?"

"It really is brilliant, isn't it? And the best thing is your contract shouldn't be a problem at all. When would be best for me to pop round?"

"Good call! I don't make any significant decisions without checking in first either. When are they in so I can explain it to them and they can ask me any questions?"

None of this is any different from any other business, people express interest and you help them to move the conversation forward.

Let me be absolutely clear. If you've left any conversation with a promise that you'll call tomorrow, next week, three weeks

Tuesday at 3pm, then you must keep that promise. It's a funny thing, and something to do with the way that humans take on information. But when you say to someone that you'll call them tomorrow, what they actually hear is that you'll call them tomorrow. I know, weird, isn't it?!

If someone has actively shown interest in what you do, then follow that through until they're ready to buy, or have decided it's a no-for-now, in which case the next section has something for them too.

Passive follow-up

Let's face it, most people don't immediately rush up to you with their debit card ready. It's a shame, and it would be great if life were different.

So, all those people who you meet, and aren't a no-for-now, just simply aren't interested, or you didn't even get round to talking to them about what you do, what do you do with their business cards?

Bin them? Because they're of no interest at all? Well, that's certainly efficient and in many ways a time saver.

Alternatively, you could, of course, use all the tools available to you, to keep gently in touch until they are in a more receptive mood, or the penny drops for them, or one of those trigger points occurs. Or just keep in touch for the sake of keeping in touch because they're nice people!

Networking gives you the opportunity to meet people at scale, and modern communications, such as social media, email marketing, and content marketing gives you the opportunity to keep in touch with them at a similar scale, notice when there are any buying signals and react by going one-to-one with the person.

What is really important is that this isn't following up on a lead, this is simply keeping in touch and allowing the other person to know what you do for a living, so that you're in the right place at the right time if they decide they might want to take a look.

The way I look at it is this. When somebody joins your network, they appear on the outer edge of your network. They have met you, they don't really know you and at this stage they have no idea whether they like or trust you.

It is now your job to help some of those people move closer to you. At this stage, the people you have met are contacts, and you need to put the effort in which will convert some of them into prospects, and some of those prospects into new customers or distributors.

It is really important to understand that people you meet at networking events **ARE NOT** immediately prospects. Far too often people go straight for the sale and then, when the sale isn't forthcoming, fail to keep in touch. Someone might not have been ready to buy then, but they may well be in the future.

So, this is how I recommend you use social media to keep in touch with business contacts after networking events.

Firstly, connect with them. Sometimes people will have their social links on their business card, sometimes you may have to go and find them. Use the search facilities on LinkedIn, Facebook, Instagram and Twitter to find them and connect with them.

Would you believe that most people don't even go this far? They rely on the other person to connect with them.

I would then send a message on your chosen platform, just to say you enjoyed meeting them and are pleased that you've connected.

By the way, if they exist on platforms that you don't 'like', you have a choice to make. You can either go to them, or expect them to come to you.

Now is the time to apply effort to strengthen these relationships. As Dale Carnegie said in his book *How to Win Friends and Influence People, "You will win more friends in two weeks by being interested, than you will in two years by trying to be interesting."*

What that means in practice is that you move onto their turf by showing genuine interest in what they're doing. On social media, it means you take the time to read their tweets, posts and articles. You check out what they're putting on Instagram. And, when you're genuinely interested, you take the time to like, comment and share.

When you do this, consistently, regularly and honestly, guess what? People then come back and look at your stuff too.

When your ratio of being interested in other people's stuff, to putting your own stuff out there is right, people will reciprocate by showing interest in what you do too. Some people will never show an interest, but enough will.

Then, when you put your own articles, tweets, pictures and even ads out there, people will be watching, because you spent the time and put in the effort to look at their stuff first.

Being genuinely interested in other people is one way of being the first in the relationship to bring value. People really do like to reciprocate, to pay back that effort, and they will.

All of my social media timelines have many more replies, comments and shares in them than they have broadcasts.

When I work with business owners, I look specifically about how this should work for them, which platforms will work for them and what strategy will work best on each one. The above gives you an overview and I completely accept there is no 'one size fits all' approach to social media, quite the opposite.

Secondly, but still about going to people rather than expecting them to come to you, is the thorny subject of email marketing.

People tell me, often, that email marketing is dead. It absolutely isn't, but it has evolved. I get open rates of around 25% on my emails and I am ridiculously flattered that so many people choose to read what I send out. Furthermore, a small proportion of the people who read the emails even click through to the links I send them.

Think about how many emails you receive? Do you read every single one of them these days? Of course you don't, it is nigh on impossible in 2018 to read every message that appears in your inbox, including the newsletters and sales emails.

So, put yourself in the recipient's place. What is going to inspire them to actually read what you send? Is an update of what you or your company has done in the last few weeks and how well the office move went going to cut it?

Once again, ensure you are constantly bringing value to the relationship. Send emails which draw attention to articles you have already written. Send emails which your audience will actually want to read.

Email marketing platforms such as MailChimp offer you the opportunity to actually see who is reading your emails and who is clicking the links you send. You can also see who has unsubscribed from your list (which isn't the insult you think, it is actually incredibly helpful information).

And most of all, pay attention. Who is actively reading and commenting on your articles? Who is opening every one of your emails? Those are the people who are moving closer to you, those are the people you should be paying special attention to, because they're paying special attention to you. Those are the people, frankly, who I would put myself in front of at a networking meeting before too long and ask them for a one-to-one.

Imagine how much information people have the opportunity to read, watch or listen to these days. And how flattering it is if they choose to read, watch or listen to yours. And how flattering it is to them if you choose to read, watch or listen to theirs.

All of this takes effort and application and, as you know, effort is currency.

Something which I am asked all the time, like several times a day, is what you should put on social media, what you should post about, what you should talk about. Something which I notice is massively understated in the network marketing world is the enviable lifestyle which anyone in their own business can enjoy. The fact that you can go to the gym whenever you like, do the school run every day, take time out for coffee with friends, and never have to ask a boss for permission, is a particularly attractive aspect of the network marketing world.

Gary Vaynerchuk often says that you don't need to come up with clever videos, social media posts and blogs. His exact phrase is 'document don't create'. Simply share with people what is going on in your life. How many people stuck in nine-to-five jobs will envy your ability to take this afternoon off just because it's sunny? Or spend more time with your kids than they do. And how many of those people might then just be interested in your opportunity on the occasions when you do post about it?

Show genuine interest in other people and then show them how genuinely interesting your lifestyle is too. Watch for the people who really are interested in what you do, and ensure you move towards them and allow them to move towards you.

Actually talking to people

With all of this social media, content and email marketing going on, I really mustn't downplay the importance of actual contact with people. Picking up the phone and actually meeting people are hugely underrated in this part of the 21st century, and you can stand out by putting the effort into meeting people in real life.

So often these days I spot people trying to run their entire marketing and sales operation by social media or email, even trying to close people using those methods. For all the advantages which social gives us, particularly the ability to engage at scale, it is so important to know when to take any conversation one-to-one and actually pick up the phone, or make an appointment to meet with them.

Effort is currency and the person who puts in the effort to take a conversation offline and continue it in real life will always be streets ahead of someone who tries to conduct the entire conversation in emojis and gifs!

Chapter 10

Joining it all up

Stefan Thomas

The last ten years or so have offered everyone in business the most incredible opportunity. What was called Web 2.0, social media, the new world of constant communication and the ability to communicate at scale has levelled the playing field more than any development in my lifetime.

Keeping in touch with our networking buddies has never been easier. The number of platforms available to promote our business has grown so much in the last few years and, incredibly, most of this amazing new opportunity is provided to us completely free of charge.

This opportunity comes with some potential pitfalls. With the chance to massively enhance your reputation comes the potential to spoil it. With the prospect of exposing your business to many more prospective customers comes the possibility that you could push people to ignore your stuff or even, the ultimate 21st century snub, to unfollow or unfriend you.

So, the 60 million dollar question, which we hope to answer in this chapter, is, how do you grasp this huge opportunity without blowing it. How do you use it to your advantage, and not just sink into invisibility? How do you sell, without selling?

We have talked lots about the Meet-Like-Know-Trust or Know-Like-Trust culture of networking, with the ultimate goal being to be someone who other people trust enough to do business with, or refer business to. This new world enables anyone to speed that process up.

A very simple way to build that trust is to have a consistent approach online and offline, in real life and in the virtual world. Just because it is inside your phone or laptop and you're posting from your dining table doesn't mean that your approach should be any different than if you had just turned up for breakfast, dressed to impress.

Often, in fact far too often, people seem to adopt an online 'persona', they're simply not the same online as in real life. People are much more likely to trust someone they can get to know, and know that they know that person, rather than finding that the person they have got to know online is different to the person they meet in real life, or vice versa. People also sometimes appear braver online than they do in real life, more willing to challenge or criticise people. If you wouldn't say it to someone's face, then don't say it online, seems to be a very good rule of thumb or, to use the age-old advice, if you haven't got anything nice to say, don't say anything at all.

Think about your personal brand, how you want to be perceived, who you want people to know you are, and make sure you show up as that person everywhere you're visible, online or offline. Be yourself, because if you try to maintain a false persona, the mask will eventually fall off.

Another aspect which seems to confuse people is that just because you can broadcast your business to many thousands of people, doesn't necessarily mean that you should.

You wouldn't, or at least I hope you wouldn't, walk straight into a networking meeting and start shouting at everyone about your business or opportunity. If you would, please go back to Chapter 1 and start again!

If you wouldn't do that in real life, why do it in the virtual world? Facebook, Twitter and Instagram are not the online equivalent of the noticeboard in your local post office. People log onto social media to chat and be social, not to be broadcast at or sold to.

As Wes always reminds us, it's called social media, not anti-social media.

Think carefully and at all times about how you present yourself in both the real life and online worlds and, as much as is possible, make sure your approach is consistent. That way, you're reliable, people know what to expect, they know you're not 'pushy', and they have the chance to get to like and trust you.

Social media, and indeed networking, can bring in quick results, but some of the bigger results come with medium and long-term effort. Sometimes it takes time for people to trust you and sometimes it takes time for people to need what you're selling, even if they do trust you.

The more I network, the more I invest in social media, the more I notice that my results are exponential, and the same for the people who I work with.

That long-term effort, being as enthusiastic three, four, five years in as you were at the beginning and putting as much effort into building your relationships now as you did five years ago can have truly massive results, which make it worth sticking at it for the long-term.

Wes and I first chatted on Twitter and kept up that relationship for at least two years before we actually spoke on the phone and then decided it would be a good idea to meet up.

In those two years Wes didn't try to sell me on his opportunity, nor did I try to sell myself to him as a speaker. We just chatted, got to know each other as people and, to use Wes' expression, became friends for the sake of being friends.

We decided to meet up for half an hour for coffee one afternoon when our paths were likely to cross and, for the first three hours of that half an hour (I know!) we didn't talk business or try to sell to each other.

We talked about stuff, we talked about what we had in common, our families, our likes, our dislikes, what we do in our spare time, and all manner of similar strands.

And now, four years after our very first conversation, I am sat here writing a book with Wes. I have spoken at his events. I have provided services to the company he partners with in the UK and I have become a customer of his too. Rather than forcing those sales at first, we allowed the relationship to mature to the extent that we trusted each other enough not only to do business with each other, but to be happy to recommend each other to our own networks too.

Just think about that for a second if you will. Wes and I have spent many years and effort building up our reputation and credibility. If either of us had tried to force the other to lend out that credibility before the time was right it could have been potentially damaging. Asking for it, may well have been the thing which convinced either of us not to give it.

Please treat all of your relationships like this. The trust takes effort, and sometimes it takes time too.

Online as well as offline you can become the 'go to' person, the person known for being helpful.

I constantly look for opportunities for my networking colleagues, that might be referrals, or it might be news articles relevant to their business which I think they can comment on, or write about, or it might be someone I think they should make contact with. I send a LOT of emails with the subject heading *"I saw this and thought of you"*. This takes me minutes every day, but the impact is huge. I always try to be the first to bring value to every relationship, something which you could easily do too.

However you show up, online or offline, be the same person, make sure your online networking and your real life networking is joined up, continue to bring value to others and you will see the results grow.

Leaders Top Tips

"I found out that your net worth is directly proportional to your network, and the brilliant thing is you get to define what 'worth' means for you, which I find really empowering.

Rather like John F. Kennedy once said, "Ask not what your country can do for you - ask what you can do for your country", in the same way, think not what your network can do for you, but what you can do and how you can serve your network.

I would say in my experience of business networking; the following five rules have helped me hugely:

1) Have a positive impact on everyone you meet and make people feel good about themselves.

2) Treat people not how you would like to be treated but how they would like to be treated by spending time to find out.

3) Be authentic - have a genuine interest in helping people.

4) Give unconditionally without thinking about what you can get in return.

5) Do what you say you're going to do when you say you're going to do it.

Chris Williams, Network Marketing Leader and Author of 'Don't Just Dream It...Do It!'

"Starting at a new networking meeting can feel a bit like you're the odd one out in the playground. Everyone knows each other and they are all laughing and enjoying themselves. It's easy to lose confidence and feel intimidated.

At least that's how I remember feeling when I first started networking. I made it my mission to spend more time getting to know them over the first few months by standing next to different people during the open networking sections and booking one-to-one sessions to find out about them. I made sure these early sessions included the people who were bringing in the most business to the room and the organisers or people who held an organisational position.

I didn't hold on to any expectation of business coming to me and made sure that I was bringing referrals to the room for them.

If there is a social event make sure you attend as that will fast-track you to creating relationships within the group. You'll soon find that you are the one laughing and enjoying yourself, and will, I hope, go over to the person who looks a bit lost and engage in conversation with them."

Kim Bradley, Network Marketing Leader

"I have taught myself to ensure that whenever someone tells me that they are looking for a service of any description, or if they mention their car needs a service or they are having a birthday party or they have a blocked drain, I say to them *'I may know someone who can help with that'*. Obviously, if I have someone in my networking group who can help, I refer them straight away. If not, I will speak to people in my group to see who they know, like and trust, and then make the connection anyway. This way I am always helping people I know, and creating value for the group I am part of."

Steve Pankhurst, Network Marketing Leader and Business Networking Chapter Leader

"For most people, their favourite subject is themselves, which is only natural. The challenge in the networking world (or anywhere where you want to build rapport) is that the other person doesn't usually want to hear all about us.

There's always at least one person at a networking meeting who turns every conversation around to them. You talk about your last holiday and they top it with a story about where they've just been. You mention a hobby they like too, like golf, and they recount their own recent experiences.

A good networker has two ears and one mouth and should use them both proportionally - building connections takes time and effort.

As a good networker, we focus on the other person. Asking open questions to get them to talk about them, their business and what they're looking for. Show a genuine interest and listen intently. While they're talking we should just be nodding and making encouraging noises, simple signs to let them know you are engaged and interested in the conversation. Your time will come, they will usually, eventually, ask about you. But by focusing on them you make them feel special.

Be interested, not interesting."

Stuart Ritchie, Network Marketing Leader and Business Networking Group Leader

"Unless your company is brand new to market, chances are that the people you meet may have met one, two or fifty-nine other people who also offer what you do! The good news is that if they want what you have, the deciding factor will be YOU, and that's something you're completely in control of.

What makes you different? What's your story? Make sure you know this, are proud of it, and then own it.

But we all know how it goes. You mention the words 'network marketing' and those not so familiar with our awesome profession will switch off. They're anticipating an over-the-top sales pitch about miracle products and a laptop lifestyle. Someone might even mutter 'pyramid scheme' into their coffee.

As tempting as it is to launch into a defensive tirade, don't. Instead, call it out before they do.

My favourite line goes something like "I know you're all waiting for my miracle product that was crafted in the Himalayan mountains by unicorns, but I'm afraid I don't have one. What I do have is ABC, which is pretty good for XYZ, so come and have a chat with me if you're open to finding out a bit more."

Lizzie Burrill, Network Marketing Rising Star

"In my earlier days in the business, I attended a lot of networking events. It was good to meet small business owners and self-employed people from all backgrounds who became advocates and referrers for me. I found that by leading with relationships rather than trying to force everyone to become my customer, made me much more referrable.

Furthermore, the networking skills I learned helped me in lots of other ways when it came to building my customer base, team and income. Understanding that by bringing value to every interaction and trying to help people, leaves you with people being much keener to help you."

Jan Whittaker, Professional Network Marketer

"There's a simple principle around helping enough people get what they want and you will get what you want. This is perfect for the modern-day networker.

I've always tried to take this approach with networking and it certainly works. Trying to be the ultimate networker essentially means you being the ultimate helper. A smile, the ability to listen to someone else's business interests and requirements, and then the selfless attempt to source contacts and referrals.

This makes you the most valuable person in the room - the 'go to' person to get things done. Be patient and this will come back to help you many times over, even if you have shared little or nothing about what you actually do!

Enjoy helping others with passion and a smile... the dividends will follow!"

Robin Brooks, Top Ranking Network Marketing Leader

"Too often we look at who is around and then make a judgement on whether this will be a good or bad day for us. What I always try and think of is that it isn't just who is around me that matters, but they each have a huge number of contacts who they might introduce me to, providing we get on well.

So, engage with everyone you meet, see who you can help and you're much more likely to become someone who gets lots of referrals."

Joga Shoker, Network Marketing Leader and Business Networking Group Leader

TESTIMONIALS ABOUT THE AUTHORS

"Some people catch you with their smile, then endear you with their thoughtful actions, kind spirit and humble heart. That's Wes Linden. He's built one of the most successful organisations by leading with a culture of friendship over business, principle over pride and caring over credentials. When Wes shares from his journey, take notes... and apply them to your journey. You'll be glad you did."

Art Jonak, Mastermind Event® founder (MastermindEvent.com), Entrepreneur and World-Class Networker

"It has been my pleasure, and to the benefit of both me and my business, to have been working with Stefan Thomas for some years now. Stefan is a rarity, he understands business networking at the strategic and tactical levels. He implements what he teaches in his own business, and with his clients. Simply put, you will not find a more accomplished person on the network, or a better ally in your business."

Phil Terrett, Director of JohnnyMuttley.com

"Throughout the years I've had the honour of meeting many of the top Network Marketing leaders in the world. Wes Linden is one of those, and to see the love and respect he has from so many in his profession is absolutely inspiring."

Bob Burg, co-author of million-seller books 'The Go-Giver' and 'The Go-Giver Influencer'

"The approach Wes takes is simple, easy to duplicate, and is based on a real understanding of human nature."

Andy Waring, Network Marketing Leader and Author of 'Make the Phone Your Friend'

"In over 10 years of running business shows, expos and conferences I've never engaged any presenter who holds the room, the audience and the topic as well as Stefan. He is not only a genius with every aspect of networking, he's a trusted advisor and confidante and I'm proud to say good friend. Nobody comes more highly recommended by me."

Andrew Charlton, Chief Executive Officer, Hashtag Business Events

"Wes delivers powerful, practical ideas that will instantly boost your bottom line, as well as increase your belief in what is possible in the network marketing profession."

Sarah Robbins, Network Marketing Leader, Author of 'Rock Your Network Marketing Business'

"I found myself in the classic situation of doing a fair amount of networking, and, although I was gaining some clients, I wasn't gaining the volume that you would expect, and I was getting a bit despondent.

So, it was time I asked Stef for help. He gave me a new strategy to use, and, within six days, I had gained a new client using it.

Stef is a genius. Don't flounder around hoping your results will improve, ask for Stef's help and get your networking working!"

Claire McTernan, Director of 'No Fluff; Just Results'

"Wes has exceptional emotional intelligence, and a strong instinct for the right response to pretty much any problem. That makes his views - based on 20 years in the industry - a 'must read' for those who want to get ahead."

Justin Bozzino, Business Development Director for a FTSE250 PLC

"I have personally and professionally know Wes for many years and his skills in networking are outstanding. He has been a brilliant speaker at many events for our company as he has the ability to fully understand this profession. Wes always has a balanced view with an in depth outstanding of how life works. He supports charitable organisations that changes people's lives. He is dedicated and loyal to our industry and highly respected world-wide. I absolutely recommend his books and understands that simplicity is the key to success."

Arthur Spurling, Managing Director for a major European Network Marketing business

"It's been said that winning and losing is often a matter of holding onto the end of the rope when everyone else is letting go. Wes Linden has produced massive results in network marketing because he held onto the rope regardless of the challenges."

Orrin Woodward, New York Times Bestselling Author & Inc. Magazine Top 20 Leader

"The training I have received from Stefan Thomas has been invaluable. It's had a dramatic effect on the success of my business and helped me achieve many networking goals.

It's simple to understand, easy to duplicate and has amazing results.

What's great about what he teaches is that it translates brilliantly from business networking environments straight into real-life too, so it has actually helped me with other aspects of my business too."

Ben Golding, Professional Network Marketer

"As a tremendous leader within the profession, Wes has mastered a way of thinking to be successful in this business."

Andrea Waltz, Author of 'Go for No!' and 'Million Dollar Year'

"Rather than get demoralised by the hype that suggests you have to be an elite performer, Wes has shown you can build a hugely successful business by putting people first in an authentic way."

Dr Tom Barrett, Author of 'Dare to Dream' and 'Work to Win' and International Speaker

"I had the opportunity to finally hear Wes speak at The Network Marketing Mastermind Event® in Orlando, and he lived up to and blew past his impressive reputation. Few speakers today talk from actual heartfelt experience and authentic truth."

Richard Bliss Brooke, Author of 'The Four Year Career' and 'Mach II, The Art of Vision and Self Motivation'

"Words are just words unless you live by them. Wes Linden walks the talk!"

Hilde & Orjan Saele, Owners of a major worldwide Network Marketing company, Author of '90 Days to Win'

"Stefan Thomas is one of greatest mentors who has transformed my life on many levels. I flew all the way from Sydney to London to learn from him the profitable art of business networking. Stefan taught me how to network with people, get meetings and sell face-to-face, which allowed me to top my game as Sydney's #1 Marketing Mentor.

What I love about Stefan is that he is very smart and understands how people feel. This translated to great lessons that I could use in my life right away.

Since his mentoring, my client base has grown by over 400% and I owe him big time. Stefan is a great guy and I LOVE HIS WORK!"

Edward Zia, Marketing Mentor, Coach & Speaker

"Wes Linden is a highly professional and inspirational network marketing leader, whose hard-working approach, warmth and willingness to support his team, have resulted in his current well-earned success. Anyone seeking to follow in his footsteps will find their chances greatly enhanced by reading this book, and following the tips and advice it contains."

The Hon. Charles Wigoder, Executive Chairman of major British FTSE 250 company

About the Authors

Stefan Thomas

Stefan Thomas is the author of Business Networking for Dummies, and Instant Networking.

Formerly he was Network Director for 4Networking and was personally responsible for running over 5,000 networking events per year.

More than that though, he is someone who has used networking extensively to grow his business and is now founder of The Networking Retreat, helping business owners of all sizes, and from across the UK and Europe, to make more sales through their networking and social media efforts.

As well as over 500 small business owner clients across the UK, Stefan is trusted by the likes of Lloyds Banking Group PLC, Telecom Plus PLC, The Chartered Institute of Management Accountants, The Chartered Institute of Securities and Investments and many other large organisations to advise and train their teams in networking skills.

He has appeared in The Daily Telegraph, The Guardian, and The Huffington Post, and is regularly asked for his opinion on changes and developments in the networking and social media world.

With a penchant for loud shirts, and even louder rock music, Stefan lives in Oxford, England, and has three sons who are his inspiration, his biggest fans and his biggest critics, all rolled into one.

Also by Stefan:
*Business Networking for Dummies
*Instant Networking

Connect with Stefan:
facebook.com/stefanthomas.biz/
instagram.com/noredbraces
twitter.com/noredbraces
StefanThomas.biz

Wes Linden

Wes Linden was a student, thousands of pounds in debt and living with his mum when he first heard about network marketing. Hoping to earn some money he decided to give it a go. After a few months, Wes was hooked and eventually dropped out of university.

Despite many of his friends and peers asking him, "When are you going to get a proper job?", Wes rode the storm and found himself financially semi-retired by the age of 24, and by 27 his residual income had overtaken the average salary of not just a teacher (the career for which he was destined), but a Headmaster.

Wes has never had a 'proper' job thanks to this profession and has only ever been involved with one networking business. He is still actively involved as a distributor, having reached the top position in the plan, with an annual team turnover approaching £100m.

In 2013, Wes became the first ever Brit to speak at the Network Marketing Mastermind Event® in Orlando, alongside the biggest network marketing names in the world. By 2015, he had been given the honour of being the host for the entire event, a role that he continues to enjoy. In 2018, he was invited to host a Direct Sales Summit in Texas, for the corporate officers of network marketing companies worldwide.

He is committed to the expansion of the profession and building its credibility worldwide. He believes this will be simpler when networkers from all companies link arms with each other. His first book '79 Network Marketing Tips' has been an Amazon best-seller in its' categories for 56 consecutive months at time of going to press.

Outside all of this, Wes is a keen traveler and has, on average, one holiday a month. He sees a personal trainer most days and recently retired from his other vocation as a football referee, where he officiated up to Championship level. He also enjoys spending lots of time with his close friends and family, and is a proud uncle to Noah and father to Coby (a Dachshund!).

Also by Wes:
*79 Network Marketing Tips For Fast-Track Success
*The Prospecting Game: How To Follow-Up & Sponsor With Confidence
*Wes Linden Chats With Randy Gage: Real-World Truths For Network Marketing Success

Connect with Wes:
Free live training videos @ facebook.com/WesLinden
Lifestyle @ Instagram.com/WesLinden
Blogs @ WesLinden.com
Podcast @ WesLinden.com/podcast

30115921R00067

Printed in Poland
by Amazon Fulfillment
Poland Sp. z o.o., Wrocław